THE BAPTISM OF POWER

ENGAGING THE CHARISMATICS, THE EVANGELICALS AND THE PENTECOSTALS ON THE HOLY SPIRIT

SAMUEL TUNDE ABEDNEGO

This publication contains the opinions and ideas of its author. It is intended to provide helpful and informative material on the subjects addressed in the publication. The author and publisher specifically disclaim all responsibility for any liability, loss or risk, personal or otherwise, which is incurred as a consequence, directly or indirectly, of the use and application of any of the contents of this book.

WORKBOOK PRESS LLC
187 E Warm Springs Rd,
Suite B285, Las Vegas, NV 89119, USA

Website: https://workbookpress.com/
Hotline: 1-888-818-4856
Email: admin@workbookpress.com

Ordering Information:
Quantity sales. Special discounts are available on quantity purchases by corporations, associations, and others.
For details, contact the publisher at the address above.

ISBN-13:   978-1-955459-07-5 (Paperback Version)
             978-1-955459-08-2 (Digital Version)

REV. DATE: 21/04/2021

Author's Email : samuelabednego301@yahoo.com

The Baptism of Power:
Engaging the Charismatics, the Evangelicals and the Pentecostals
Pentecostals
on the Holy Spirit

Dedication

To the glory and honor of Christ Jesus, the Son of the
living God, and to the body of
Christ worldwide.

Endorsement

Churches (and especially, the evangelicals) all through the years are developing the souls of people but neglecting the minds. This has been one of the major problems in Christendom. This author now emphasizes both, that is, to develop the soul as well as develop the minds of the Church members. The writer provides a balance Theology in that he presents an engagement that rally round the development of both the soul and the mind. He claimed that both the revelation-knowledge of God as well as the academic knowledge of God are needed. But beyond that, he emphasizes the place of the Holy Spirit in getting the revealed truths about God and His words for daily transformation. It is based on the soundness of this position that I recommend this author and the book to Christians worldwide. Dr. A.T. Samuel's book is a worthy voice added to existing ones.

Stephen Oluwarotimi Y. Baba, PhD

Professor of Biblical Studies

Former Provost, ECWA Theological Seminary, Igbaja

Member, Board of Trustee, Development Associates International.

Acknowledgment

My profound gratitude goes to God Almighty for the love, faithfulness, mercy, and generous grace that He has bestowed upon me. Through His beloved Son Christ Jesus, who shed His blood on the Cross for the forgiveness of my sins, God raised me out of the ash heap and made me a partaker of His love and mercy together with all of the redeemed. He made me worthy of being called His son. To Him be all glory forever.

This book is based on my dissertation for my doctoral study at The Southern Baptist Theological Seminary (SBTS), Louisville, Kentucky, a great citadel of knowledge that the Lord has used as a quarry for my remaking and remolding. This book copiously quotes Zac Poonen, an amazing man of God whose teachings have tremendously benefited the growth of my faith. Poonen freely permits the use of his work, provided that the user first applies it to teaching himself or herself and that Poonen is accurately quoted.

I am very grateful to Professor S.O.Y. Baba, a reputable man of God and former lecturer at ECWA Theological Seminary, Igbaja, Nigeria, for investing time in reviewing the manuscript of this book. My gratitude also goes to Bishop Ponle Alabi, of Covenant of Peace Evangelistic Association Inc., whose demonstration of outstanding qualities has been an inspiration to me, even as God continues to use him for noble purposes globally.

I am likewise indebted to Rev. Adeyemi O. Ibikunle, of East Audubon Baptist Church, Louisville, Kentucky, who significantly contributed to the restructuring of the initial draft of my manuscript for local and global relevance; Elder Michael Jolayemi of California and Bro Shedrach Adamu, who skimmed through the manuscript; Dr. Joshua Odetunde, an excellent man of passion who was an inspiration for the work; Pastor Roger Scott, one of my adopted fathers in the United States, with whom I experienced the demonstration of the miraculous hand of God on several mission trips; Roger and the entire membership of the Least, the Last and the Lost Ministry; Linda M. Wilke, who edited my manuscript and witnessed to the transformative effect of the work on her life; David Olawoyin, who also helped in editing; Jennifer Briggs, who proofread the manuscript and added a unique flavor to it; Eld Joseph Jide Omotinigbon, who helped at one point on a document editing; Torey Teer (at SBTS), who meticulously reworked the draft, and Mom Eleanor Stevens and her friends, who were of tremendous help to this writing project. I am immensely appreciative of you all. In addition, thanks to the Jack Gupton family, Dean Clerke family, Tony Kennedy family, Mom Shirley Moskovich, and the Men Bible Study group at Hike Point Christian Church, Louisville KY for their continuous supports.

My darling wife, Peace, has always been a divine encourager and resource to tap into. Her wisdom, Spirit-filled life, and immense contribution undergird the success of this work. I could not have come this far without her support. Our children—Temple, Gospel, and Miracle—are also divine instruments and fellow prayer partners who have unquantifiably contributed to my journey.

FOREWORD

The Holy Spirit represents the presence of God with the disciples of Jesus Christ and is promised to always abide with them. However, teaching about the Holy Spirit has been neglected in many churches, resulting in the average Christian's having little knowledge about this divine personality. Some Christians believe that the experience of the Holy Spirit is about being emotional or under an inexplicable strange influence. However, the Holy Spirit is the Spirit of truth, our counselor, and our advocate. He is the Spirit of Jesus Christ who quickens the body of Christ. While some Christian denominations embrace all biblical truths about the Holy Spirit, including His fruits and gifts, others only accept some. Generally, all denominations agree on the fruits of the Holy Spirit, but the gifts remain controversial.

In this book, Dr. Samuel Tunde Abednego explains all that we need to know about the Holy Spirit, including who He is, how He operates, and what the attitude of the Christians toward Him should be. Dr. Samuel is a Bible scholar, and his present exposition of the subject of the Holy Spirit is both simple and passionate. The work represents a balance between his personal encounter with the Holy Spirit and a theological study of the subject. This book promises to benefit Christians, non-Christians, church leaders, theological students, and members of Bible study groups. It can also be used as a personal devotional or for group study.

It is of utmost importance for Christians to have a proper understanding of the Holy Spirit and to develop an intimate relationship with Him. According to Jesus, sinning against the Holy Spirit is the only transgression that is unforgivable. The Holy Spirit is gentle and holy, even though He works through men and women created from dust. Nevertheless, they are the only creatures whom God has chosen to accommodate His Spirit.

Adeyemi Ibikunle
Pastor, East Audubon Baptist Church
Louisville, Kentucky

Preface

Before beginning a lecture on pneumatology, which is the area of theology that deals with the Holy Spirit, a seminary professor asked his graduate students two questions. The first was "How many of you have heard a teaching about the Holy Spirit?" About 90 percent of the students indicated that they have not received teaching about the Holy Spirit. The second question was "Whenever the Holy Spirit is mentioned, what comes to your mind?" Various answers were given: "something scary," "a ghost," "something transcendent," and more. Unfortunately, some of these students would attend one or two such classes on the Holy Spirit to pass a semester exam, go on to graduate from the seminary, and then head for mission's fields to serve as pastors, teachers and missionaries! This shallow knowledge of the Holy Spirit, as well as the lack of a personal experience with Him, is one of the reasons for the failure of some Christian missions. In addition, churches are becoming lifeless because many pastors do not have an intimate relationship with the Spirit of Christ.

I have observed that many of my evangelical friends try to avoid any discussion about the Holy Spirit and His gifts. Things get worse when I talk about the sign gifts (such as speaking in tongues, prophecy, healings, knowledge etc.) of the Spirit. I have experienced stigmatization and have faced multiple panel inquiries for believing that these gifts of the Holy Spirit are still in operation today. My question is Why should we talk about the fruits of the Spirit (Gal 5:22-25) and not His gifts as well (1 Cor 12:1-12)? If the Spirit whom the early believers received is the same Spirit who presently indwells us, then why are we in conflict about His operation? Where are we really getting things wrong?

Conversely, some of my Pentecostal friends, out of pride and ego, consider other Christians who do not speak in tongues as carnal and immature. However, in some churches that claim to have the power of the Holy Spirit because of their glossolalia experience (i.e., speaking in tongues), the leaders are enslaved by the love of money and materialism. Some measure the power of the Holy Spirit by material accumulation or the level of display of the sign gifts. Despite all of these contradictions, we all need the Holy Spirit's fruits, gifts, and manifestations of the power in order to enjoy a wholesome Christian experience.

Part of the purpose of this book is to appeal to professing Christians of all shades—charismatic, evangelical, Pentecostal, etc.—not to let what Christ intended for our good to create enmity among us. With humility, we can learn from one another and work together as one body of Christ. In this book, I also highlight the existence of counterfeit spiritual gifts in the church today. Ultimately, it is my hope that you would discover that God's power can truly work in and through you for effective Christian service. This book is intended to enable both academic study and a practical and devotional approach to understanding baptism with the power of the Holy Spirit, which is available to every believer of Jesus Christ. It is my earnest desire that every reader would experience the awesome presence and power of the Spirit of God for victorious Christian living and productive witness to the world. Those who walk with Christ look like Christ. In this book, you will discover the mystery of walking with God the Holy Spirit before working for Him.

Samuel, Tunde Abednego
Doctor of Missiology

Chapter 1

We Need the Baptism of Power

"But you will receive power when the Holy Spirit comes on you; and you will be my witnesses in Jerusalem, and in all Judea and Samaria, and to the ends of the earth" (Acts 1: 8)

Encounters with the Holy Spirit among different church denominations and individual Christian are viewed in various ways. People give different names to their encounters with the Spirit. Some call it 'second experience,' 'second work of grace,' 'the infilling of the Holy Spirit,' 'the fullness of the Holy Spirit,' 'baptism of the Holy Spirit,' 'anointing of the Holy Spirit,' and the likes. However, regardless of whatever nomenclature you hold to, something is very certain; we need the 'baptism of power' from the Holy Spirit. The Evangelical, the Orthodox and the Pentecostal Christians should all know that we cannot fully grasp the total operation of the Holy Spirit here on earth. With all our 'pneumatology' (the doctrine of the Holy Spirit), we can only know in part. The Holy Spirit is God. In the Scripture, the prophet Isaiah says, *"With whom, then, will you compare God? To what image will you liken Him?* (Isaiah 40:18, 25; 46:5).

If we, with our finite and fallible knowledge, can understand all that has to do with the workings of the Spirit in totality, then the Holy Spirit is less than God. It is like calling on a dog to explain the psychology of human being. Because of its extra sensory perception, a dog may be able to perceive that his owner loves him. A smart dog can be trained to perform certain skills. In fact, some dogs can be taught some elementary mathematic concepts such as additions and subtractions. But when it comes to multiplications, algebra, matrixes, a dog becomes a novice. No dog can explain how the brain of any man functions. Much more, the margin between us and God is wider beyond that of man and a dog. The description above fits into what every scholar or writer on the Holy Spirit has been doing for centuries. We can all write according to the revelations we all received, and therefore, we must be humbled enough to admit that we do not know all (1 Cor 13: 9, 12).

Again, the Holy Spirit is God, and we cannot fully explain his workings through the best of our human academic abilities. To try and explain the ministry of the Holy Spirit fully would be as foolish as one dog trying to explain human behavior to another dog. All that a dog may be able to say to another dog is this; "I do not know anything about human psychology. But I do know that my master is very kind to me. He takes good care of me—and I am very happy". A dog can experience his master's goodness, but he cannot explain his master's psychology. So it is with us and the Holy Spirit. We cannot explain his activity fully, but we can experience his love, his goodness, and his power—and this is enough. No mortal man can fully theologize or able to explain all of the workings of God the Holy Spirit.

Let me use this short illustration to describe the blindfold the devil has put on many in Christendom. Due to this blindfold, millions of Christians have failed to tap into this available power. I am presently living in Louisville, Kentucky. Supposing a man is sent on an official assignment from Louisville to Texas. Available for this man are a bicycle, a motor bike, a four-wheel auto car, and a flight ticket. But in his ignorance, this man decided to let go the offer of traveling by flight or any of the other options but decided to travel by a bicycle. Of course, if he decided to ride to Texas on a bicycle, he would definitely get there, but a lot of time and energy will be expended. It was like Moses who in his passion was planning to kill the Egyptian army with bare hands one by one, which would have taken him thousands of years to do. But when Moses had an encounter with the power of God, he drowned all the Egyptian army in a single day just by lifting his 'rod' over the Red Sea. You need the power of the Holy Spirit. It is non-negotiable if you want to live a victorious Christian life and serve God effectively. Regardless of what your spiritual calling and ministry is, until you are clothed with power from on high through the Holy Spirit, you cannot be effective. If you run short of this power of the Spirit in your life, you need to desire it passionately. You need to ask for it. You need to thirst for it, and you need to receive it. This power is available.

Which Side of the Cliff are you?

According to Zac Poonen, if the devil does not want you to be baptized with the Spirit's power, there are two ways he will go round it. With regard to the power of the Holy Spirit, there are two groups of people both falling on the different sides of the Cliff. There are those going to the extreme of fanaticism (like those who claim that you are not genuinely born again until you can speak in tongues). So, this group becomes highly emotional and speaks some gibberish even though they are still slaves to sins. Secondly, there are still other God-fearing people who tell themselves, "We do not want to have anything doing with this whole bunch of gibberish or anything with the charismatic move of the Holy Spirit". Hence, whenever anybody speaks about the power of the Holy Spirit around them, they turn to themselves saying, "We need to be careful about this guy!" The first set of people falls on the other side of the Cliff; and this later group that are reacting also falls on the opposite side of the Cliff. The devil is quite happy with both groups because he has succeeded in turning them away from receiving the real thing that Christ has come to give them.

Is there a benchmark for the right position on what it means to be filled with the Holy Spirit? Yes! Consider the life of Jesus Christ— whom we look up to as our perfect example. Though 100% God, when he came to the world as a man, the Holy Spirit had to come upon him so that he could live a victorious life without sin and be able to fulfill his ministry effectively. He lived and worked by the power of the Holy Spirit. Hence, we need this power too! Furthermore, the life of the early apostles of Jesus Christ as we shall see in the pages of this book is worth emulating.

Chapter 2

The Emptiness of Dependence on Head Knowledge

"He has made us competent as ministers of a new covenant—not of the letter but of the Spirit; for the letter kills, but the Spirit gives life" (2 Cor 3:6).

As different scholars try to point out the different errors especially among today's Charismatic movement, Pentecostalism and neo-Pentecostalism,[1] the tendency of falling into intellectual or academic Christianity remains as a trailing danger among bible scholars (especially among the evangelicals). We really need not to seek for theological degrees to impress people, but rather to ultimately arrive at the point of divine revelation that leads to maturity in Christ. When Jesus began his ministry, he chose unlearned fishermen to put to shame the great scholars of his days. Gamaliel was a seminary professor; Ananias and Caiaphas were like archbishops then. But Jesus hand-picked Peter, James and John who were local fishermen by the Sea of Galilee and turned them out to be his apostles who will be the foundational members of the New Covenant. He did this in order to reveal the emptiness of the cleverness of men in the religious circle of his days.

---

[1] I have written about these in my next Book tittle, "Nigerian Neo-Pentecostalism: A Glimpse into African Modern Christianity." (The manuscript of this book is on the queue waiting for publication any moment from now).

These men chosen by Christ were men of little academic knowledge in terms of human standard in their days. They were so much uneducated that the scholars of their days tagged them *'agramantos'*—meaning 'unschooled' or unlearned. *"Now when they saw the boldness of Peter and John, and perceived that they were unlearned and ignorant men, they marveled; and they took knowledge of them, **that they had been with Jesus** (Acts 4:13).* Christ found out these men that were considered as nobodies; he anointed them with the Holy Spirit and used them powerfully. God always works in this way then and now because, an intelligent man who serves God with his scholastic prowess may fall into temptation of thinking that God is using him because of his cleverness—and brag of it.

These early apostles of Christ got the revelation-knowledge of God and the perfect understanding of spiritual things. Nevertheless, living with Jesus and learning from him for three years have so much impacted them as they literarily lived out the life of Christ that demonstrated that they have really being with Christ (Act 4:13; 11: 26). It is important to know that in the New Testament way of life, we know God more by revelation and not by academic ability. Revelation in this regard is the unveiling of the truth about God and His word which our finite mental knowledge cannot reveal to us but by the illumination of the Holy Spirit in accordance to the balanced word of truth—that is, the Scripture.

Today, highly learned scholars are trying to understand most of the things that are written or done in the Scripture by ordinary fishermen. With all the available tools like lexicons, commentaries, concordances and other scholastic materials, we have still not been able to lay hold on the Power that moved the apostles and the early believers to achieve all they achieved through the Gospel. With all our theological and Bible schools, we also seem not to be as godly as they were. I am not against theological degrees; they are very vital for making the work of church leader easier. As a matter of fact, in my thirst and hunger for God, I have gotten my own share of the theological degrees. However, my succinct conclusion even with doctoral degrees, is that to understand the scriptures, you need to read with the heart of a child not the mind of a scholar.

Of course, God is not against intellectual ability—he makes use of several clever and intelligent people. For instance, Paul was privileged to learn under the renowned Rabbi Gamaliel. No doubt, Paul was a formidable genius and an erudite scholar of the law. If he were to be alive today, he could have been the best guru in the world of science or the best attorney of his generation. But Paul did not depend on any of his abilities in serving the Lord. He allowed the message of the cross to crucify his human confidence and qualifications. To the Corinthian Christians, Paul remarks, *"For I resolved to know nothing while I was with you except Jesus Christ and him crucified"* (1 Cor 2:2). His preaching was not a display of human cleverness, but the demonstration of the power of the Holy Spirit, so that the faith of his audience would not rest on human wisdom (1 Cor. 2:4). Luke was likewise a man of sound intellectual capability, but no single writer of the scriptures that wrote about the place of the Holy Spirit's power like Luke did. With his intellectual prowess, he wrote two volumes of scriptures, but his writings demonstrated a life of a person who is filled with the power of the Holy Spirit and a man who had crucified the flesh. Christian Scholasticism is an empty mental display if the fullness of the Holy Spirit is missing.

The revelation-knowledge of God operates differently from the academic knowledge of God. Hundreds of scholastic minds have missed out the transformative power in the Word of God for mental pursuit of degrees on the Bible. In Mathew 11:25, Jesus said, *"Father, I praise you that you hid these things from the wise and the intelligent and revealed them to babes*". The great truths of the New Covenant have been hidden by God. You cannot discover them by academic analysis. You can read all the commentaries in the world, but you will not discover them, because they are spiritually coded – hidden from the clever and the intelligent. Man has tried to know his creator through intellectual means, but this has proven impossible because God can be known only through revelation that comes through intimacy with the Holy Spirit and the word of God. You need revelation and God gives that only to those who are like babes—who have pure hearts. Whether they have a clever head or not does not matter. [2] Smartness and intelligence give us no advantage whatsoever in God's kingdom if we have not been broken by the Holy Spirit. It is a pure heart that gets God's revelations. Children are teachable; a little child is ignorant and gladly accepts that.

My little boy, Gospel, once asked, "Daddy, why is it that trains do not travel on the same road with cars?" As an adult, I know that, but a child does not know even a simple thing like that; and a child can be very honest about it. Only few believers come to God

---

[2] Zac Poonen, *Through the Bible: A Message for Today from Every Book of the Bible* (Bangalore: CFC, 2016), 556.

in a humble and meek way like that saying, "Lord, you wrote this Book; what does this mean? I am foolish in spiritual matters. Please explain it to me." In the New Covenant, we have the privilege of being filled with the Holy Spirit and to have him teach us the Scriptures that he himself wrote (1 John 2:27). No wonder the apostle Paul prayed for the Ephesians saints for divine revelation for them. *"For this reason, ever since I heard about your faith in the Lord Jesus and your love for all God's people, I have not stopped giving thanks for you, remembering you in my prayers. I keep asking that the God of our Lord Jesus Christ, the glorious Father, may give you the Spirit of wisdom and revelation, so that you may know him better. I pray that the eyes of your heart may be enlightened in order that you may know the hope to which he has called you, the riches of his glorious inheritance in his holy people, and his incomparably great power for us who believe"* (Ephesians 1:15-19).

Truly, Christ has appointed teachers in the church. You will never know God if you stop only with what you receive by listening to those teachers. What they teach you may be true, but you get it second hand from them. We have to be wise like the believers in Berea (Acts 17:10-11). Whatsoever word of truth you might have received from any preacher or teacher, you have to take that word before the Lord, saying, "I want to know you personally Lord." Then the Holy Spirit will shed light on those truths for your personal revelation. Because of our direct access to God on individual basis in the New Covenant, the Scripture says, *"this is the covenant that I will make with the house of Israel after those days, saith the Lord; I will put my laws into their mind, and write them in their hearts: and I will be to them a God, and they shall be to me a people: And they shall not teach every man his neighbor, and every man his brother, saying, Know the Lord: for all shall know me, from the least to the greatest* (Hebrew 8:10-11).

Listening to Poonen sometime ago, I heard him telling the story of a young man some years ago who graduated from a Bible college. He came first among the graduating students and won many prizes (best student in Greek, best student in Hebrew, best student in theology, etc); and was set to become a local church pastor. After hearing the exaltation message from the invited guest speaker, he went to the speaker secretly telling him how he was thoroughly defeated by sin in his inner life throughout his years of studies. He confessed to him that, after four years of all his studies, he was worse than when he came into the Bible College. The question is, how was all his Bible knowledge going to help him when he became a pastor? Was he going to teach people the root meanings of the Hebrew and Greek words in the Bible? That's not people's greatest need. People want to know how to overcome sins in the innermost place. This is the tragedy in Christendom today. There are several theological professors, students in Bible colleges, pastors and teachers in churches who are still living in sins, in lusts, ego, pride, addicted to pornography, addicted to substances, engrossed in sexual promiscuities, unforgiveness, and the likes; yet they are preparing to go and teach others. R. Albert Mohler once said, "a sinner who comes to saving faith in Jesus Christ already knows more than any academic theologian who doesn't know Christ."

Bible scholars armed with numerous degrees are teaching people theories that do not work in daily life to make people become like Christ. Consider Paul, a man from a wealthy background in Tarsus. Tarsus was a town where Jewish businessmen went to do business. Again, in his young age, Paul had gone to the best seminary in Jerusalem—where the scholarly Gamaliel was the professor. It was a great honor to study under such a professor. Hence, Paul did not just come from a wealthy community; he also had a brilliant mind. But he did not depend on any of these abilities to serve the Lord.

To the Corinthians Paul said, "*When I came to you proclaiming the testimony of God, I did not come to you with superiority of speech or wisdom.*" His preaching was not with words of human cleverness or eloquence, but in the demonstration of the power of the Holy Spirit, so that people's faith would rest on God's power and not on human cleverness (1 Cor 2:1-4 NIV). When you preach the Word, make your preaching very simple so much that little children can understand you. Jesus spoke in a very simple way, even children could understand him. Make sure you are not preaching to impress the clever ones but to bless all the people that listen to you. If you want to help people, be simple in your speech. God reveals His truths to those who have a heart like a little babe and not to those who are proud of their intelligence and their scholarly degrees.

Hence, Paul was essentially saying, "even though I have a brilliant mind and I am a great scholar and could have used all that to speak to you, I did not do that. I laid everything at the feet of Christ—all my ability, my knowledge, and my scholastic prowess. I decided to speak to you in a very simple way with the power of the Holy Spirit so that the Holy Spirit could take my words home to your hearts and not to your minds alone. I do not want to impress you with my cleverness; I want the Holy Spirit to bring conviction into your hearts and to lead you into the way of abundant life in Christ". This is the word of the Cross.[3] Approaching the subject of this book with this kind of mindset will help every reader to grasp the truth that the Lord wants to pass across to all. I am not writing as a scholar, but as a toddler in the things of the Spirit. I am writing as one who constantly trembles under the mighty Hand of God.

---

[3] Poonen, *Through the Bible: A Message for Today from Every Book of the Bible*, 691.

Chapter 3

Getting to Know the Holy Spirit

"But very truly I tell you, it is for your good that I
am going away. Unless I go away, the Advocate
will not come to you; but if I go, I will send him to
you"
(John 16: 7)

I will try as much as possible not to bore my readers with

endless debates and arguments on the Holy Spirit that have plagued

the body of Christ for centuries. Much more most of the New

Testament (NT) scriptures are written by nonprofessional and even

unlearned fishermen. But today, it takes scholars countless number

of debates and argument to understand what these simple men had

written. The reason simply is; we need the humble heart of a baby

to get the revelational truths that God wants us to see in the

Scripture. Prolific and erudite writers have argued on what the

'baptism of the Holy Spirit' really is (Acts 1:5), and when does this

baptism really take place.[1] Similar to these is the expression 'filled

---

[1] The Pentecostals believe that the baptism of the Holy Spirit is the
second work grace which happen subsequent to conversion and goes along with
the evidence of glossolalia (speaking in tongues). The Charismatic has the same
concept of the baptism in the Holy Spirit similar to the Pentecostals, but do not
hold that speaking tongue is a convincing sign of the baptism of the Spirit. For
more, see Wayne A. Grudem, ed., *Are Miraculous Gifts for Today: Four Views*
(Grand Rapids, MI: Zondervan Publishing House, 1996), 10-11. To many
evangelicals, the baptism of the Spirit goes along with the Christian conversion;
it is not a second work of grace, it is not subsequent to salvation, and speaking

with the Holy Spirit.' Regarding the different schools of thought, the emphasis of this book aligns ultimately with Peter Wagner point of view when he writes,

> Issues such as whether we are baptized or filled with the Spirit once or many times, whether it occurs at conversion or subsequent to conversion, or whether there is initial physical evidence to certify that it happened, are more important to some Christian leaders today than others. But we will all agree: We need to receive the supernatural power of the Holy Spirit in our lives and our ministries to the greatest extent possible to serve God well in our world.[2]

Misconceptions about the Holy Spirit have been debated since early church history. For instance, in AD 325, Arius was condemned as a heretic for his belief that the Holy Spirit was only an influence emanating from the Father (God).[3] As a matter of fact, the Holy Spirit is the most misconstrued person of the Godhead. Some denominations see him as the unseen guest—something like a vapor with fluid inside. The Pentecostals see him as a vital force that motivates speaking in tongues with great emotional display. The Charismatic believers see him as a worker of miracles, signs,

---

in tongue is not required as a proof. See Graham, *The Holy Spirit: Activating God's Power in Your Life*, 32-3
    [2] C. Peter Wagner, *Acts of the Holy Spirit* (Ventura, CA: Gospel Light, 1982), 55.
    [3] Wayne Grudem, *Systematic Theology: An Introduction to Biblical Doctrine* (Grand Rapids: Zondervan, 1994), 243.

and wonders resulting into diverse manifestations like falling under the power (slain in the Spirit), whereas, some other groups see him as a dove, water, a feeling or fire. However, contrary to some of these descriptions, the Holy Spirit is not a force that makes people fall out, not an emotion, a fire, a dove, or water—He is God. Throughout the Scriptures, the Holy Spirit is portrayed as a being or a personality with intellect, will, and emotion. In addition, Jesus places the Holy Spirit as equal with the other persons of the Godhead.[4]

As Wayne Grudem asserts, "The Holy Spirit is fully God."[5] Once one understands God the Father and the Son to be fully God, then Trinitarian expressions (such as seen in Matt 28:19) "assume significance for the doctrine of the Holy Spirit, because they show that the Holy Spirit is classified on an equal level with the Father and the Son."[6] For instance, regarding the personality of the Holy Spirit, Scripture often uses the pronoun "he" for the Holy Spirit (John 16:7, 13). The Holy Spirit is also described as a being with an intellect (1 Cor 2:10). Many scriptural verses confirm this truth. As

---

[4] Bruce A. Ware, *Father, Son, and Holy Spirit: Relationships, Roles, and Relevance* (Wheaton, IL: Crossway, 2005), 41.

[5] Grudem, *Systematic Theology*, 245.

[6] Ware, *Father, Son, and Holy Spirit*, 41.

with the other members of the Trinity, the Holy Spirit is omniscient (1 Cor 2:10-12), omnipotent (Job 33:4), and omnipresent (Ps 137:7-10; John 14:17). He possesses all the attributes of God. Thus, the presence of the Holy Spirit is indispensable in the life of every believer. He is on the earth "to manifest the active presence of God in the world, and especially in the church—which the Scripture most often represents as being present to do God's work in the world."[7] Hence, Christians cannot do spiritual work effectively if they do not understand the place of the Holy Spirit in that work. The Holy Spirit is here to manifest the nature of Christ through every Christian and to do in us and through us the works of the Father. The misconception on the Holy Spirit is not limited to his personality alone; there are scores of arguments about his operations either as a result of semantic usage or due to theological imbalances. Let us dive into some synonymous terms for better clarification. These terms include, baptism of the Holy spirit, immersion in the Holy Spirit, and the filling or fullness of the Holy Spirit.

Baptism, Filling, or Immersion in the Holy Spirit?

There have been three distinctive waves of the Spirit from late nineteenth century until now. The first wave is the Pentecostal

---

[7] Grudem, *Systematic Theology*, 635.

movement, characterized by the powerful ministry of the Holy Spirit in the realm of miraculous manifestations that some Christians found to be abnormal or unusual. "Prominent among the miraculous works were what have been called the baptism in the Holy Spirit, speaking in tongues, healing the sick, and casting out demons."[8] In this regard, and different from the second and third waves of the Holy Spirit, Pentecostals argue for a second work of grace after conversion, which they term "the baptism of the Holy Spirit," a work subsequent to regeneration (new birth) and evidenced by speaking in tongues. Concerning the first wave, Wagner writes,

> The majority of the Christians were not prepared for this outpouring of the Holy Spirit. For one thing, they had no theology for handling it. For many, the miraculous signs and wonders that we read about in the New Testament were restricted to that period of history . . . Because there was no theological grid for understanding what the Holy Spirit was doing through the Pentecostal movement; evangelicals did the only thing they knew how: They declared Pentecostals heretics.[9]

Although the Pentecostals have their own share of errors, not everything they do and believe constitutes heresy. I really will

---

[8] C. Peter Wagner, *The Third Wave of the Holy Spirit: Encountering the Power of Signs and Wonders Today* (n.p.: Servant, 1988), 16.
[9] Wagner, *The Third Wave of the Holy Spirit*, 16.

not go out of my way to some of the erroneous beliefs and practices as to maintain my focus.

The "Charismatic movement" is the second wave of the Holy Spirit. As a fulfillment of the dream of Pentecostals, the Charismatic movement broke out in the twentieth century from among the mainline denominations. [10] Though second-wave proponents look into the Scriptures with evangelical lenses, they also validate the relevance of the miraculous working of the Holy Spirit for Christianity today. Charismatics believe in the baptism of the Holy Spirit and speaking in tongues; but they never see the baptism of the Holy Spirit as a second work of grace subsequent to salvation, nor do they maintain that speaking in tongues is evidence for such a work.

The third wave of the Holy Spirit comes from among evangelicals who, for one reason or another, have chosen not to be identified with either the Pentecostal or the Charismatic movements. This last group simply retains the name 'Third

---

[10] Wagner, *The Third Wave of the Holy Spirit*, 17. Such denominations include the Roman Catholic Church as well as Protestant churches (e.g., Episcopal, Lutheran, Presbyterian, United Methodist).

Wavers.'[11] Emerging in the 1980s, Third Wave proponents believe that the gifts (including the sign gifts) of the Holy Spirit are very relevant for today church and are needed for effective witnessing.[12] They never see speaking in tongues as a must gift for all believers, but they maintain that the Holy Spirit gives gifts as he wills. Some of the champions of the Third Wave include C. Peter Wagner, Charles H. Kraft, John Wimber, Dick Bernal and others.[13] Nonetheless, regardless of their different views, all three are committed to one Body, one Spirit, one hope, one Lord, one Faith; one God and Father of all (see Eph, 4:4-6). All of them hold a high view of the authority of Scripture and believe in the urgency of world evangelization. All are convinced that the power of God described in the Gospels and Acts is in effects as God's kingdom is manifested around the world today. The similarities are much greater than the differences. But there are important differences, for

---

[11] Harvey Cox, Fire from Heaven: The Rise of Pentecostal Spirituality and the reshaping of Religion in the Twenty-First Century (Cambridge: Da Capo Press, 1995), 281-2.

[12] For more, see Wagner, *How to Have a Healing Ministry in Any Church* (Ventura, CA: Regal Books, 1988), 15-17. The argument of this Book maintains the fact that God may choose to interfere in the ways he wants as men and women take the gospel to the unreached parts of the world. However, the normativism of sign gifts as they exactly were in the days of the early believers lacks substantial biblical supports and proofs.

[13] See more in Cox, Fire from Heaven, 283-5; and Wagner, The Third Wave of the Holy Spirit, 16f.

each group feels that God has chosen to minister through them in a particular way.[14] Hence, all sense of superiority and inferiority must be discarded.

When Jesus promised to send "another Comforter" (i.e., the Holy Spirit), to the believers; his goal was not to create a division in his body, the church. Unfortunately, today, the body of Christ is divided into various factions based on the various positions concerning the person, work, and gifts of the Holy Spirit. Regarding the miraculous gifts of the Holy Spirit, there seems to be three prominent positions. The first is the "cessationist" position, which maintains that the signs and miraculous gifts of the Holy Spirit are for the early apostles and, therefore, ceased upon the completion of the New Testament. The second position is the "continuationist" view, which maintains that all the gifts of the Holy Spirit, as well as the miraculous power portrayed in the New Testament, are meant for today. They are also called non-cessationists. The third position is the "open-but-cautious"[15] view, which argues for the possibility

---

[14] Wagner, *How to Have a Healing Ministry in Any Church* (Ventura, CA: Regal Books, 1988),18.

[15] For more oncessationist and continuationist views, readRichrd B. Gaffin, *Perspectives on Pentecost: New Teaching on the Gift of the Holy Spirit* (Philipsburg: Presbyterian and Reformed Publishing Company, 1979), 109; Thomas Schreiner, *Spiritual Gifts: What they & why they Matter* (Nashville, TN: B & H Publishing Group, 2018), 165.

that miracles can and do still happen today according to how God purposes things to be by His own sovereign will. However, this third position is primarily concerned with how to curtail the potential abuse of biblical truths.[16] (I however do not want to go in depth into these routes of arguments for the purpose of focus).

Gregg R. Allison identifies two major baptisms that believers do participate in at one time or the other in life, namely, water baptism and Spirit baptism. For the two types of baptism, he identifies four elements that are critical to each. Water baptism has (1) the pastor as the baptizer, (2) the new convert as the baptizee, (3) water as the medium, and (4) the purpose of indicating one's confession of faith, incorporation into the church, membership with Christ, and obedience to the Scriptures. Spirit baptism has (1) Jesus as the baptizer; (2) the new convert as the baptizee, (3) the Holy Spirit as the medium, and (4) the main purpose of adding a new convert to the body of Christ (as reinforced by the Apostle Paul in 1 Corinthians 12:12-13 and in several other passages of the Scripture).[17] For this second baptism, Allison maintains that the

---

[16] Robert L. Saucy, "An Open But Cautious View" in *Are Miraculous Gifts for Today?* 97-103

[17] Gregg R. Allison, "Baptism with and Filling of the Holy Spirit," *Southern Baptist Journal of Theology* 16, no. 4 (2012): 8.

baptism occurs as sinners believe in Jesus Christ for salvation. It is therefore very clear at this point that no one can belong to the body of Christ without being baptized into this body by the Holy Spirit. Hence, salvation and baptism (the baptism of the Holy Spirit) take place simultaneously; there is no delay after salvation for the baptism of the Holy Spirit, which, as some take it, is to be received by the laying of hands. [18] Billy Graham writes,

> I am convinced that many of the things some teachers have joined to baptism with the Holy Spirit really belong to the fullness of the Spirit. Thus, the purpose of the baptism with the Holy Spirit is to bring the new Christian into the body of Christ. No interval of time falls between regeneration and baptism with the Spirit. The moment we received Jesus Christ as Lord and Savior we received the Holy Spirit. He came to live in our heart. [19]

The Apostle Paul says, "And if anyone does not have the Spirit of Christ, they do not belong to Christ" (Rom 8:9c), and, "No one can say Jesus is Lord, except by the Holy Spirit" (1 Cor 12:3). My argument remains therefore, that every believer is baptized into the body of Christ at the point of conversion: "For we were all baptized by one Spirit so as to form one body—whether Jews or Gentiles" (1 Cor 12:13). Even though I believe the operation of the

---

[18] Zacharias Tanee Forum, *You can receive the Baptism into the Holy Spirit Now* (Lagos: Conquest Communication Ltd, 2007), 45-64.

[19] Billy Graham, The Holy Spirit: Activating God's Power in Your Life (Waco, TX: Word, 1978),71.

gifts of the Holy Spirit-including the sign gifts, I humbly disagree with the position that sees the baptism of the Holy Spirit as a second work of grace which comes subsequent to salvation and is evidenced by demonstration of some sign—speaking in tongues.[20] This is simply because, this same baptism in the Holy Spirit is the baptism into the body of Christ. (Some may want to argue though that the baptism into the body of Christ by the Holy Spirit is not the same as the baptism of the Holy Spirit). I do believe in the infilling of the Holy Spirit which most time triggers the manifestation of different gifts.

When people first receive Christ as Lord and Savior, many do not realize the Holy Spirit at that point lives within them, but rather, they go around looking for somebody to lay hands upon them to receive the Holy Spirit. Various scriptural passages in the book of Acts have been lifted out of context to support this practice. As new believers come to know Jesus better and yield themselves increasingly to him, their desire of the flesh begins to wane gradually, and the personality of Christ begin to dominate, and the

---

[20] Late Byang Kato, a renowned African theologian once said, "young Christians today are being urged to seek "a second blessing" or a "second baptism" especially among the Pentecostals. This kind of teaching defies thorough and true biblical interpretations." See, Byang Kato, "The Power of the Holy Spirit," in *Today's Challenge* (Jos: Challenge Publication, September/October 1974), 4.

34

Spirit is giving more space to fill. Some call this later experience of the Holy Spirit's work a 'second blessing' or the baptism of the 'Holy Spirit.' The more of yourself you yield to the Spirit, the more of you is immersed in the Spirit. However, the Bible calls this the filling of the Holy Spirit. As believers hear, receive and apply the truth of the Bible; the Holy Spirit may fill us, not simply a second time, but again and again.[21] Nevertheless, for those who go either by the baptism of the Holy Spirit or those who go by the 'filling of the Holy Spirit,' one thing is certain: we all need the Power of the Holy Spirit. And when you truly encounter this power of the Spirit, you will know you have it. Hence, there is no need to quarrel over semantic or linguistic issue.

Just as the apostle Paul clearly says, *Don't be drunk with wine, because that will ruin your life. Instead, be filled with the Holy Spirit* (Eph 5:18), Allison's explanation on the filling with the Holy Spirit is very instructive. According to him, a person may be indwelt by the Spirit of God but may not optimize the inherent blessings of the Spirit until a later time in life. He goes on to point attention to the examples of people who were already indwelt by the Spirit but were uniquely filled at particular times so that they could perform

---

[21] "Preparing for Pentecost," BSF notes on Act 1 September 2019.

certain unusual tasks. In the book of Acts, these examples include Peter (4:8), the Jerusalem church (4:31), Stephen (7:55), Paul (13:9), Barnabas, and others. To be constantly "full of the Holy Spirit" brings every Christian to a state of being effective, fruitful, and productive in life and in fulfilling the Great Commission. Wayne Grudem, in accord with Allision, presents four notable and practical marks or works that the fullness of the Holy Spirit produces in a yielded life: empowerment, purification, revelation, and unification.[22] Hence, my argument remains that the continuous filling of the Holy Spirit is needed for continuous empowerment, and this empowerment is vital for effective evangelism. More remarkably, the baptism of the Holy Spirit takes place at the point of regeneration, but the continuous filling of the Holy Spirit produces power in believers for victorious and effective Christian living.

Two things that worth differentiation

Again, there is still a need to differentiate between two most misconstrued phenomena in regard to the operation of the Holy Spirit in Christendom from decades past till now. First, is the gift of the Holy Spirit; second, the fullness or infilling of the Holy Spirit.

---

[22] Grudem, *Systematic Theology*, 635.

The gift of the Holy Spirit: The Holy Spirit comes in on the day a sinner repents and embraces the gospel. The Apostle Peter in his preaching after the day of Pentecost said: *"Then Peter said unto them, Repent, and be baptized every one of you in the name of Jesus Christ for the remission of sins, and ye shall receive the gift of the Holy Ghost"* (Acts 2:38). No one can say Jesus is Lord except by the Holy Spirit (1 Cor. 12:3). The Holy Spirit comes to seal every believer in Christ Jesus. The scriptures say, "in whom (Holy Spirit) ye also trusted, after that ye heard the word of truth, the gospel of your salvation: in whom also after that ye believed, ye were sealed with that Holy Spirit of promise" (Ephesians 1:13). With this same gift of the Spirit, everyone who believes in Christ is baptized into Christ's body. Jesus once said, *"The least in the kingdom is greater than John the Baptist"* (Matt 11:11). Throughout the Old Testament, there was no one who had the Holy Spirit residing inside of him or her permanently. The least may be the one who has just received Jesus into his life (who is yet to reach the full stage of maturity or one who is weak spiritually). Such a person has the Holy Spirit residing inside of him or her which none of the OT saints had. This new covenant kingdom is not a matter of eating and drinking, but righteousness, and peace, and joy in the Holy Spirit (Rom 14: 17).

The fullness of the Holy Spirit (Being filled with the Holy Spirit): This is what I think the Pentecostal and Charismatic movements place much emphasis upon and tagged it as the 'baptism of the Holy Spirit.' On the Day of Pentecost, it is evidently seen that the believers were all baptized into the body of Christ. This unique day was the day the third person of the Holy Spirit came to the world to indwell believers—the body of Christ.[23] His coming to the world was accompanied by wonders and unique manifestations. *"And when the day of Pentecost was fully come, they were all with one accord in one place. And suddenly there came a sound from heaven as of a rushing mighty wind, and it filled all the house where they were sitting. And there appeared unto them cloven tongues like as of fire, and it sat upon each of them. And they were all filled with the Holy Ghost, and began to speak with other tongues, as the Spirit gave them utterance"* (Acts 2:1-4). Right from this moment, the Holy Spirit does not need to come from heaven again.

Although, there are few places in Acts we read about the dramatic interferences of the Holy Spirit in the lives of those who

---

[23] Nevertheless, some have argued that Jesus breathing on the disciples in John 20: 21-22 saying, "receive the Holy Spirit" and breathing on them is the joining to the body, and the other is the infilling or fulness. But my response to this will be, what about others among the 120 believers who were not present there when Jesus breathed upon the twelve, but who together with the twelve received the Holy Spirit on the Day of Pentecost?

were just receiving salvation in the name of Jesus Christ for the first time (besides the repentance in the order of John the Baptist) if we read contextually (cf Acts 10:42-45; 19: 1-5). Hence, since the day of Pentecost, the Holy Spirit has been living inside everyone who received Jesus Christ; the Spirit has *'tabernacled'* on earth, and there is no need to tarry again for the Holy Spirit to come down from heaven. But as you continue to read the Book of Acts, even after being baptized into Christ's body on the day of Pentecost, there are several places you will find that the apostles were said to be filled with the Holy Spirit (Acts 4: 31; 7:55; 9:17; 13:9). The filling with the Holy Spirit is a continuous occurrence in the life of every believer. The continuous filling led to the fullness of the Holy Spirit—the power baptism, or the immersion in the Spirit. Better still, to be filled with the Holy Spirit is to be filled of the Spirit's presence and power in full capacity. It is to be totally submerged and immersed in the power of the Holy Spirit. Again, there is one baptism, but many fillings. There is no such thing as one time filling. We always need to depend on God for continuous filling. When you are filled to the capacity, there will be no space for bitterness, depression, anger, unforgiveness etc.

For proper biblical interpretation, the 'fullness of the Holy Spirit' is the same as 'the immersion in the Holy Spirit'. The Greek word for baptism is the same as 'immersion.' The word 'baptism' which was firstly used for John the Baptist really means to be 'immersed.' John the Baptist can as well be called John the 'immerser.' At the highest level of our relationship with the Holy Spirit, we are immersed in him—being immersed in the river of the Spirit's presence. The Apostle Paul admonishes, "*Do not get drunk with wine, for that is debauchery, but be filled with the Spirit*" (Ephesians 5:18). This can be compared with being drunk in the Spirit so much that just as the venom of hot wine drives a drunkard, and he is no longer in charge of himself; the Lord wants us to be so drunk in the Spirit so much that he become the controller of our moment-to-moment decisions in life. The imperative phrase 'be filled with the Spirit' also means 'be being filled with the Spirit' or 'be continually controlled by the Spirit.' "*For as many as are led by the Spirit of God, they are the sons of God*" (Romans 8:14). Jesus operated in this level throughout his life because, John the Baptist testified that the Spirit was poured upon Jesus without measure (John 3:34).

The prophet Ezekiel also revealed the level of encounter with the Holy Spirit. When the river of the Spirit engulfs us, our feet are detached from the earth and we lose our grip to the earthly things and begin to float in the direction of the waves of the Spirit's river (47:1f). John in his Gospel give us clearer understanding of this experience of immersion. *"In the last day, that great day of the feast, Jesus stood and cried, saying, if any man thirst, let him come unto me, and drink. He that believeth on me, as the scripture hath said, out of his belly shall flow rivers of living water. But this spake he of the Spirit, which they that believe on him should receive: for the Holy Ghost was not yet given; because that Jesus was not yet glorified"* (John 7: 37-39). Hence, to be baptized into the body of Christ at the point of regeneration is different from the continuous in-filling of fullness of the Spirit. The continuous filling produces power for our victorious living and effective services. I adopt the phrase 'the baptism of power' for this phenomenon. Not everybody receives this fullness of the Spirit on the same day they are converted. As a matter of fact, only few receive this alongside with their salvation experience; and that as God wills, but more pathetic to say, most believers never receive this baptism of power throughout their lifetime as a result of ignorance, negligence, or satanic delusion.

I believe that God always allow us to thirst for this fullness of the Spirit as part of the instruments to break us. This was what Jesus was referring to when he said; *"If ye then, being evil, know how to give good gifts unto your children: how much more shall your heavenly Father give the Holy Spirit to them that ask him?"* (Luke 11:13). In this scripture, Jesus does not mean that believers need to beg before the Holy Spirit is given, but for the fullness of the Holy Spirit wherein lies the power to set the captives free, we need to seek the Father's face for this. The narrative of Jesus from verse 5 through verse 9 of Luke 11 confirms it. Looking into the context of this Luke chapter 11, every believer needs to continue to ask for the fullness of the Spirit until one has gotten an assurance that he/she has received it. At this point, you are asking for power to set another person free from the bondage of darkness or you are asking God for the fullness of the Spirit to fulfill your calling and purpose on earth. I will throw more light on this passage in another chapter.

In summary, Baptism in the Holy Spirit (that is, baptism into the body of Christ) happens once at conversion. But the immersion in the Holy Spirit can be instantaneous with conversion or later. This immersion (or filling) can be done by God on automatic instances (in rare cases) or received by asking for it. That we are all baptized by the Spirit means we all have received the gift of the Spirit with which we are baptized unto Christ body. The fullness of the Spirit may come immediately or later, depending on how much of yourself you yield to the Holy Spirit. When you have this fullness, you will know that you have it. It cannot be mistaken for anything. The Baptism of power is the immersion in the Holy Spirit—that is, the fullness of the Holy Spirit.

The fullness of the Holy Spirit is needed for two major things in the life of Christians. First, you cannot live a victorious life, where you have victory over sins without this fullness. Second, you cannot totally fulfill your purpose or calling on earth without this baptism of power. Your level of immersion in the Holy Spirit will determine the level of the anointing (the functional power) of the Holy Spirit upon your life. The question at stake is, how much of you is yielded to the Holy Spirit? It is in the yielding of ourselves to the Holy Spirit that ushers in the flow of power. Hence, throughout this book, wherever the phrase 'baptism of the Holy Spirit' is used (except otherwise stated), I am referring to the fullness of the Holy Spirit, the immersion in the Holy Spirit or the baptism of power. Note again, the baptism of the Holy Spirit that Pentecostals or Charismatics speak about is the same as the infilling of the Holy Spirit, the fullness of the Holy Spirit, or the baptism of power (as I coined it here). It is good to begin with seeing the operations of the Holy Spirit in the Old Testament. Those whom God used at one point and the other in the Old Testament time all had some kind of encounters with the power of the Holy Spirit.

Chapter 4

The Power of the Spirit in the Beginning

*"When you send your Spirit, they are created, and
you renew the face of the earth" (Ps 104: 30)*

Sinclair B. Ferguson tried to demythologize the mystery that surrounds the person of the Holy Spirit in his argument. In his effort to disprove the position that the Holy Spirit is distant and impersonal, he referred extensively to both the Old and New Testaments to buttress his view. Ferguson affirms among other things that the immanence of the Holy Spirit, and as the acts of the Holy Spirit transcend the New Testament even though it is evident that the Holy Spirit became more exemplified in the New Testament. [1] The Holy Spirit featured enormously in the Old Testament too. Many passages of the Old Testament contain prophetic declarations that found fulfillment in the New Testament. The presence of the Holy Spirit at creation is such an undisputable one. Ferguson's remark in line with this assertion that the "Scripture hints that God's Spirit has been engaged in all of his works from the beginning."[2]

---

[1] Sinclair B. Ferguson, *The Holy Spirit. Contour of Christian Theology* (Illinois: InterVarsity Press, 1996), 17-8.

[2] Ferguson, *The Holy Spirit. Contour of Christian Theology*, 18.

Right from the book of Genesis, the inevitable presence of the Holy Spirit has been at work. The entire Scripture begins with, *"In the Beginning God . . . and the Spirit of God . . . and God said (the Word) . . ."* (Genesis 1:1-3). At this point, it is easy to see the mission of God the Father in the creation. But beyond any iota of doubt, the role of the Spirit in the mission of God is not hidden; the Spirit of God renews the face of the earth. The Spirit was co-creator with the Father and the Son (Psalm 104:30; John 1:1). To this, Grudem called him the "eternal Spirit,"[3] who has been before the creation of the world.

Again, the phrase "let us make man in our image, according to our likeness ...." (Gen 1:26) has poised several arguments among biblical scholars. Some have deduced that the idea of "let us" is a direct call and appeal to some heavenly beings who were likely present with God at creation. These primarily could have been inclusive of the Son and the Holy Spirit. To this, Thomas Geoffrey states emphatically that "the Spirit of God was present in and above creation."[4] To lend credence to his assertion he added that "by the

---

[3] Ferguson, *The Holy Spirit. Contour of Christian Theology*, 18
[4] Geoffrey Thomas, *The Holy Spirit* (Grand Rapids: Reformation Heritage Books, 2011), 16

Holy Spirit, Jehovah spoke the universe into existence. By the Spirit, God brought into creation the light, order, and fullness that now surrounds us."[5] More so, the psalmist expressed the role of the Holy Spirit at creation saying, "*When you send your Spirit they are created* (Psalm 104:30). Hence, God never work in isolation without the Son and the Spirit. They are in perfect unity—an epitome of team players.

Fact remains that in the Old Testament, God the Father is always seen in action with regard to his relationship or dealing with Israel, kings and nations, and scores of individuals as well. Nevertheless, we see the Spirit of God empowering individual, group of individuals, prophets, and some others for the task of missions that God was preparing them for. For instance,

- In Pentateuch as well, the Spirit came upon the seventy appointed elders of Israel and they prophesied (Numbers 11:25f).

- The Spirit of the LORD came upon Othniel in power, and he went to war to deliver Israelites (Judges 3:10)

- The Spirit of the LORD came upon Gideon in power, and he went to deliver the Israelites from their enemies (Judges 6:34).

- The Spirit came upon Jephthah in power, and he went to fight for Israel (Judges 11:29)

---

[5] Thomas, *The Holy Spirit*, 16.

- The Spirit usually descended upon Samson with power in the form of 'on and off' to fight battle (Judges 13:25; 14:6,19; 15: 14, 19).

- The Spirit of the LORD came upon Saul as he prophesied—confirming his calling, in power to fight with the Ammonites (1 Samuel 10:6-11; 11:6).

- As soon as David was anointed, the Spirit of the LORD began to move him with power (1Samuel 16:13). As a prophet and king, David knew the inevitable roles of the Holy Spirit in his life when he said: *"Do not cast me from your presence or take your Holy Spirit from me"* (Ps 51:11).

- To Zerubbabel, the temple builder, God sent his prophet with the message: *'Not by might nor by power, but by my Spirit,' says the LORD Almighty* (Zech 4:6).

Therefore, it is very clear that throughout the Old Testament, God did not give anyone a mission to accomplish without empowering the person with the power of His Spirit for the assignment. However, though the Holy Spirit was seen at work in the Old Testament, the New Testament makes the Spirit's impact in missions clearer. George W. Peters, one of the scholars in the field of Missiology said, "it is evident from the pages of the Old Testament and the Gospels that there never was a time when the Holy Spirit was not present in the history of mankind . . . His omnipresence is well attested . . . He indeed, is God who is here."[6] Thus, from the Era of Old Testament, prior the birth of New

---

[6] George W. Peters, *A Biblical theology of Missions* (Chicago: Moody Press, 1972), 300.

Testament, the indispensable role of the Holy Spirit in God's mission and the life of individuals whom God ever gave specific assignments, has been evidently seen.

From Genesis 1, the Scripture begins by pointing our attention to the move of the Spirit of the living God. If you carefully read Genesis 1, you will discover that God never spoke the 'Word' until the appearance of the Spirit upon the surface of the water. May I also add that, right there in Gen 1: 1-3, we see the activity and unity of God the Father, the Son (the Word), and the Spirit. The power that brings the entire creation into being is the power of the Spirit of God. Hence, beyond our academic prowess, we need the revelation of the Holy Spirit in understanding the Scripture which its author is the Holy Spirit Himself (2 Pet 1:21); and we need him in our daily work with Christ. As we have noted, everyone God uses in the OT was endowed with supernatural power to fulfill the tasks or the assignment given to them by God. God will not send anyone on errand at the person's own expenses or power. Adam, with God's power and wisdom, singled-handedly named every creature. Before his fall, Adam was operating at the same mental frequency with God. He was a co-regent with God, and God never finds a single fault in Adam's nomenclature. When God called Abraham to leave his people and to go to where he would show him, God empowered him for the journey to the yet unknown destination. Abraham was indomitable anywhere he went. With just three hundred home-trained men, he conquered the enemies because God was with him (Gen 14: 14).

King Pharaoh attested to the wisdom of God's Spirit in Joseph when he said; "And Pharaoh said to his servants, can we find a man like this, in whom is the Spirit of God?" (Gen 41:38). In the wilderness, God empowered Moses and gave him the staff of authority to display the supremacy of his power before Pharaoh and in the entire land of Egypt, and also to demonstrate the awesomeness of God's majesty before the people of Israel as they journey to the land of Canaan. No one was able to stand in battle against Moses. It was the same thing with Joshua as he took up the mantle of leadership from Moses (Joshua 1:1-9). Whenever and wherever a person or people stand to witness for God throughout the OT, it is always with the display of the magnificent power of God. If the OT saints were not so presumptuous to go out to witness for Yahweh, how much more do we need his empowerment for us to be able to witness effectively for Him too? To this, Jesus said, '*you will receive power, when the Holy Spirit come upon you. . ..*'

(Acts 1:8). You cannot confront the world with its powers, principles, and systems (the kingdom of darkness) without God's power. No one can successfully face the principalities and cohorts of darkness without this baptism of power of the Holy Spirit (Ephesians 6: 10-12).

The Spirit at the Threshold of the New Testament

According to R. Albert Mohler, "There are many similarities between the Gospel of Luke and the book of Acts."[7] For instance, both books focus on how Jesus fulfills the Old Covenant and ushers in the New Covenant. The two books draw attention to the person and work of Jesus. Both books draw the attention of readers to the church—the people of God who are identified not by circumcision but by faith in Christ Jesus. Both the Gospel of Luke and Acts reveal the sovereign power and purpose of God.[8] In addition, both books point attention to the ministry of the Holy Spirit. As a matter of fact, Luke never waited until he wrote the Book of Acts before introducing readers to the third person of Trinity, the Holy Spirit, who is vital for the New Covenant life. Rather, Luke's Gospel opens at the beginning by revealing the power of the Holy Spirit. Right from the beginning, Luke pointed out:

---

[7] R. Albert Mohler, *Acts 1-12 for You* (n.p.: Good Book, 2019), 7.
[8] Mohler, *Acts 1-12 for You*, 7-9.

- John the Baptist would be filled with the Holy Spirit from the womb (1:15). This connotes that John would be under the influence of the Holy Spirit; but not being a permanent residence of the Holy Spirit, since the Blood of the new covenant had not been shed yet.

- Mary would have the Holy Spirit come upon her to conceive Jesus (1:35)

- Elizabeth and Zechariah were with the Holy Spirit (Lk 1:41, 67)

- Simeon had the Holy Spirit upon him, he got revelation from the Holy Spirit and was led by the Holy Spirit to the temple (Lk 2:25-27).

- God anointed Jesus with the Holy Spirit and power and he went about doing good and setting people free from satanic oppressions (Lk 4:18; Acts 10:38)

- The disciples would receive power when the Holy Spirit come upon them (Acts 1:8)

- Paul's preached the gospel with the demonstration of the Spirit's power (1 Cor 2:1-5).

At this point, it seems Luke begins to reveal what the New Covenant life will look like—a life in the Spirit. Regardless of several arguments on the baptism, filling, fullness or anointing of the Holy Spirit, what you received when you are immersed in the Spirit is power; the reason I decided to title this book 'The Baptism of Power.'

Chapter 5

The Litmus Tests for the Baptism of Power

*"But the fruit of the Spirit is love, joy, peace,
forbearance, kindness, goodness, faithfulness,
gentleness and self-control. Against such things
there is no law" (Gal 5: 22-23).*

There are some significant marks that characterize a man that is being filled with the Holy Spirit. If you have encountered this power baptism, these things will become evident in your life. In this chapter, I will point out a few of them, and in another chapter where I discussed how to receive the baptism (chapter 13), I will add more. This chapter and that chapter will be interwoven. However, if anyone tells me he has been baptized with this power, what I look out for as evidence is his victory over the desires of his flesh and the passionate desire to witness for Christ at any moment. Anywhere you see the Spirit appearing in the Bible, you see power mostly associated with it. And this power manifests itself in diverse ways.

Victory over sin

The New Testament began with the main purpose why Jesus came. *"And she shall bring forth a son, and thou shalt call his name Jesus: for he shall save his people from their sins* (Matthew 1:21). Salvation (deliverance) from sin is different from forgiveness of sin.

For instance, when a man accepted Jesus, all past sins are forgiven instantly. If the same person falls into sin of anger ten times in a day and comes to Jesus to ask for forgiveness ten times, Jesus will forgive him. If he goes back to pornographic sites ten times in a day to satisfy himself with lust of all forms, then comes to Jesus to ask for forgiveness ten times, Jesus will still forgive him. But his life's pattern is such a cycle of going to sin and coming to ask for forgiveness. This type of man, though he receives forgiveness of sins, he is yet to be saved from sin.[1] This man needs to be honest by saying, I have known Jesus as the one who forgives me my sins, but I am yet to accept him as the Savior that saves me from my sins. The man needs the power of the Holy Spirit to break the sinful life pattern by yielding himself completely to the Spirit. The first thing that happens to you when you are filled with the Holy Spirit is a life of victory over sin (Romans 6:14). I am not talking about sinless perfection here at all, but you will hate all forms of unrighteousness with passion (Hebrew 1: 9).

A man full of the Holy Spirit is not being controlled by conscious or intentional sin. One time when my wife was serving as a youth corps member in our country (this is, a compulsory one-year

---

[1] Zac Poonen, Message on "All that Jesus Taught."

national service required of all university graduates in Nigeria), a particular well-known Church denomination organized a night prayer (vigil) program for its corps members on an open lawn (field). This is a denomination where everyone speaks in tongue as evidence that they have received the baptism of the Holy Spirit. Unfortunately, early in the morning, the field where these believers had their all-night-prayer (with so much noises and tongues) was littered with used condoms. It was evident that after the prayers (which stopped at 3 am), many of them also engaged in sexual pleasures. This matter brought reproach to the Name of Christ among the unbelieving corps members serving in that batch.

When I was growing up as new covert in Christ, I also witnessed similar thing when students in some schools' fellowships would organize baptism of the Holy Spirit programs and laid hands on people to receive the Holy Spirit with the evidence of speaking in tongues. Yet, these same brothers and sisters were always seen caressing one another and engaging in many forms of sexual immoralities at various corners on campus. Some were caught in the act of immoralities; some impregnated themselves and went for abortions. There are proponents of Pentecostalism who are leaders, pastors, deacons, elders and many evangelical professors of theology who claimed to be filled with the Holy Spirit; yet, they are not free from these atrocities. With all their knowledge of Bible, they are still slaves to sins. Regardless of whatever the display of charismatic gifts or head-knowledge of the Scripture, a man is not filled with the Holy Spirit yet, if he is still a perpetual slave to the lusts of the flesh. Hence, different from the way the Spirit of God came upon people in the Old Testament to fight wars, today; the Holy Spirit does come upon believer to perform certain assignment to the Lord's glory, to overcome the giant of lustful desires and to witness to the gospel effectively.

Righteousness above the righteousness of the Pharisees

Jesus says, "For I say unto you, that except your righteousness shall exceed the righteousness of the scribes and Pharisees, ye shall in no case enter into the kingdom of heaven" (Matthew 5:20KJV). The righteousness of the Pharisees was of a higher standard. For instance, the Pharisees prayed at least two times in a day, they fasted regularly, gave tithe of all forms, engaged in witnessing and proselytism, followed the traditions of the elders etc. Was Jesus telling us to go and do double of the activities that the Pharisees were doing? No. But Jesus actually came to raise the bar of living, but not in the direction of the righteousness of the

Pharisees. Many people today are still in the category of the old Pharisees as they boast about the size of their church buildings, the number of people in their congregations, the number of times they pray and fast in a week, the amount they give as offering and tithes, the number of countries they have traveled to, the number of books they have written, the number of their material possessions, their financial worth, etc. But Christ's emphasis in Matt 5:20 is not on quantity of our activities but the quality done not by human power, but by the help of the Holy Spirit. Hence, what does Jesus mean when he says here, "if you want to enter the kingdom of Heaven, your righteousness must exceed that of the Pharisees?" In what way?

There were two commendable things about the Pharisees, and Jesus alluded to these. First, as far as doctrinal issue is concerned, the Pharisees got a lot of things right. *"The teachers of the law and the Pharisees sit in Moses' seat. So you must be careful to do everything they tell you. But do not do what they do, for they do not practice what they preach"* (Matt.23:2-3). Jesus did not say this about the Herodians who were worldly, nor about the Sadducees who did not believe in the resurrection (plus some other doctrinal errors). In a paraphrase, Jesus said that the Pharisees had a correct doctrine. Second, Jesus declared that ". . . *You clean the outside of the cup and dish* . . . (Matt 23: 25). So, the Pharisees had a faultless external righteousness. Hence, externally, they were faultless before the Law of Moses. Now, do you believe that someone can have a 'correct doctrine' with a faultless external life and still be in danger of hell? Jesus said yes! (Matt 23:33). In the Old Testament, so far you did not commit adultery in the physical, you are not guilty before the law. But in his teaching on the beatitudes, Jesus said, a lust (strong desire in your heart) after an opposite sex is a sin already. The same thing goes with murderer. Jesus expatiated that anger is the seed of murder, so anger sitting in your heart is the same as committing the sin of murder (Matt 5: 20-22).

The truth that liberates. Let us take a little glimpse from the teaching of Jesus on the beatitudes to appreciate how the fullness of the Holy Spirit can help us to overcome sin in our lives. With the Spirit's baptism comes the law of life (not the Mosaic Law) that sets free from the law of sins and death (Rom 8:1-2). The righteous requirement of the law is now fulfilled inside of us because we no longer walk in the flesh; we walk according to the leading of the

Spirit which was impossible under the law. Hence, the whole teaching of Jesus Christ in Matthew 5-7 was something impossible for any man to do under the law without the power of the Holy Spirit. Mathew 5-7 reveals to us the standard of life God expects of the people in the New Covenant. For us who are born-again, our righteousness must surpasses that of the Pharisees. The teaching in Matthew 5-7 was proclaimed by Christ to create a desire in our hearts for this type of life. And if anyone has a longing for this type of life, he will go to God and say, "Lord, I cannot fulfill all these teachings of yours. What is the solution?" And the Lord will reply, "you need to be filled with the Holy Spirit, you need to be strengthened in the inner man." The Apostle Paul was able to keep the external laws perfectly and was blameless before the law. But as far as the inward lusts and covetousness are concerned, Paul was honest to confess that he falls short until the Holy Spirit came with a new life of victory (cf. Philippians 3:6b; Romans 7:23-25; 8:1-2).

There are lots of counterfeit experiences of the baptism of the Holy Spirit today, which only emphasizes speaking in tongues; but the inner life of victory or freedom from sin is not emphasized. Yes, I am not against speaking in tongues, but the fullness of the Holy Spirit brings something far more important; the deliverance from sin is the primary purpose of the fullness of the Holy Spirit. The baptism of the Holy Spirit whereby people roll on the ground, laugh and yell, yet they are still overpowered by unforgiveness, sexual lust, immorality, love of mammon (money), endless covetousness for materialistic things, dominated by anger—wherein they shout at their spouses and staff, is merely a soulish counterfeit baptism. If this has been your experience, do not let anyone deceive you with this counterfeit baptism; go to God and seek for the real baptism. When we are baptized in the Spirit's power, the Holy Spirit gives us a new tongue (not just speaking in an unknown tongue). There is no use of speaking in an unknown tongue on Sunday morning in the church and come back home in the afternoon to shout at your spouse in your mother tongue—that is not the baptism of the Holy Spirit.

Self-control in various areas

The fullness of the Holy Spirit gives us control over our tongues, because the fruit of the Spirit is self-control. He gives us control over our tongues 24 hours a day, and 7 days a week; if it is not that, then ask God to give you a genuine baptism of the Holy Spirit. Glory be to God for the gifts of the Holy Spirit, but you need to ask God for the genuine fullness or power baptism. The Holy

Spirit will give us control over our tongues and eyes. Jesus spoke extensively on sinning with the tongues and the eyes in Matthew 5: 20-32. If the baptism of the Spirit you received does not give you victory over sinning with your tongues and with your eyes, you need to go before God and say, "Lord, I got a cheap counterfeit baptism, and have been fooling people around that I got a baptism of the Holy Spirit because I speak some gibberish. Now Lord, I need the original baptism, I do not want to miss out on the genuine fullness of the Holy Spirit."

When I was once overpowered by sexual lust, I started moving from one fellowship to another seeking for the baptism of power through the Holy Spirit. But in most places, what I saw were empty noises; and I said, Lord, this is not what I am looking for; I'm looking for power to overcome sin. I told God, if this is going to take me years, I will wait for it. I want what the apostles got that helped them to overcome sins and to fulfill their callings; I'm not after the cheap counterfeit baptism that many have for sale in the market today. God did saw my honest and passionate heart, and he allows his Spirit to engulf me; he gives me victory over my sinful lusts. The devil wants people to be satisfied with the counterfeit and settle for it. Do not be deceived to settle for pseudo-baptism. You cannot be a lover of money and say you are baptized in the Holy Spirit. There are many that are baptized by mammon, and yet they speak a lot of gibberish and accumulate a lot of material things in the name of anointing of the Holy Spirit.

Passion for the lost souls

The second evidence of this baptism is the passion for evangelism. I'm not talking about people who are committing sin and yet still witnessing. We have seen people who indulged in immoral affairs with their so-called converts. I'm also not speaking about those who are witnessing because of the financial and material gains that will come to them as they present their reports with inflated statistics of converts and events. There are those who are also witnessing for some selfish purpose ranging from the quest to be known, to be promoted or to be rewarded. Jesus scolded the Pharisees on their damaging missional activities when he said, *"What sorrow awaits you teachers of religious law and you Pharisees. Hypocrites! For you cross land and sea to make one convert, and then you turn that person into twice the child of hell you yourselves are!"* (Matthew 23:15 NLT).

Most time, when you are overwhelmed in your spirit about the eternal damnation waiting for the lost, then you begin to hear the cry of the souls of men and women that are heading toward the tunnel of hell, and your heart begins to beat in love and passion toward rescuing them. I cannot remember the number of times I have wept in my spirit, and loudly as well, whenever I see the number of people unwittingly heading to hell as they die without Jesus. To begin with, looking at the lives of the early disciples of Jesus, they were all a bunch of coward people prior to the day of Pentecost. But immediately when the Holy Spirit came upon them in power, they became as bold as lion in witnessing for Christ. The Holy Spirit changed ordinary cowards to fiery witnesses for Christ and changed the directions of their lives forever. Ware expressed that "the gospel of Jesus would go forth as the Spirit of Jesus would empower the proclamation of Jesus."[2] In the same school of thought, David Platt writes, "While every Christian wants to experience the power of the Holy Spirit, we often forget that the Spirit's power is given for the purpose of being his [Christ] witnesses. Experiencing God, which is the longing of every true believer, happens when we are being his witnesses and making

---

[2] Ware, *Father, Son, & Holy Spirit. Relationships, Roles, & Relevance*, 113.

disciples."[3] The purpose of the Spirit coming upon the disciples is to empower them to bear witness about Christ from Jerusalem and beyond (Acts 1:8). The Spirit indeed gives power to the believers to testify effectively to the gospel. After they prayed, Luke clearly writes, *"With great power the apostles continued to testify to the resurrection of the Lord Jesus. And God's grace was at work so powerfully in them all"* (Acts 4:33). The Holy Spirit indeed empowers the church for the global evangelism.

In Luke 15, Jesus told a parable that has to do with passion for the lost or backsliders. It is a parable of three losses—a lost sheep, a lost son, and a lost coin. We see the shepherd as the picture of Jesus searching for the lost sheep. The father with a lost son is a picture of God the Father who never for once stopped seeking for the erring son to come back home. The woman who lit up the candlelight searching for the lost coin is a picture of a church that is filled with the Holy Spirit and searching for the lost souls. You cannot remain as a nominal Christian again when you are immersed in the Spirit. This power will push you out of your comfort zone. I used to be a quiet, easy-going and the introvert type until I received

---

[3] David Platt, *A Call to Die. A Call to Live: Follow Me* (Carol Stream: Illinois; Tyndale House Publishes, 2013), xvi.

this touch of Power. The passion for the works and the things of the Lord engulfed me as soon as I got a glimpse of this Power. This is different from religious commitment or a mere participation in dead works; it is investing your life toward things of eternal value.

Becoming more and more like Jesus

The third ultimate purpose of the power baptism that I want to mention here, for every believer, is to become more and more like Jesus Christ in our daily life. The Holy Spirit is given to us so that we can become conformed to the image of Christ in our daily life (Romans 8: 29). In Luke 1:34-35, we read how angel Gabriel responded to Mary's question by saying, *"The Holy Spirit will come upon you, and the power of the Most High will overshadow you."* Again, the Holy Spirit always brings to us the power of God (Acts 1:8; 10:38). Until the Spirit produces Christ in us, there will not be a release of power. As the Spirit of God came on Mary to produce Jesus in her, so the Spirit comes upon us primarily to produce Christ in us. This is the clearest guideline you can have to understand the ministry of the Holy Spirit in our life and in our service for the Lord. As it took time for that body to grow inside Mary's womb;

sometimes, it may take time for Christ to become manifest in our lives.[4]

The duration of time depends on the measure of our submission, yielded-ness and brokenness. There are lot of pseudo-manifestations of 'power' today through men and women in whom there is no evidence or fruit of the life of Christ. In the next two chapters, I will elaborate the more reasons why we need this power baptism. I will begin with how Jesus Christ himself was duly anointed, and I will also delve fully into how it is a must to be endued with power before we can become effective witnesses of the Gospel. Baptism of power that goes with ego, pride, arrogance, love of money and the likes is definitely a counterfeit baptism. Hence, the full fledge of the fruit of the Spirit characterizes a genuine baptism of this power. *"But the fruit of the Spirit is love, joy, peace, forbearance, kindness, goodness, faithfulness, gentleness and self-control. Against such things there is no law"* (Gal 5: 22-23). At the fullness of this baptism is the place where God reveals His Son in me and through me by the Holy Spirit.

---

[4] Poonen, *Through the Bible: A Message for Today from every Book of the Bible*, 585.

Chapter 6

How God anointed Jesus Christ with Power

*"How God anointed Jesus of Nazareth with the
Holy Spirit and with power, who went about doing
good and healing all who were oppressed by the
devil, for God was with Him" (Acts 10: 38)*

During the baptism of Jesus Christ (Luke 3:21-22), Luke's

record unveils the significant impact the descent of the Holy Spirit

upon Jesus had in his witnessing task. For example, reading further,

Luke says that Jesus, full of the Holy Spirit, left the Jordan and was

led by the Spirit into the wilderness (4:1). Then, Jesus returned to

Galilee in the power of the Spirit (4:14). Right at the beginning of

his public ministry, Jesus announced that the scope of his missional

task was to preach the gospel to the poor, heal the brokenhearted,

preach deliverance to captives, preach recovery of sight to the blind,

give liberty to those who are oppressed, and preach the year of the

Lord's favor (4:18-19). Each of his duties required strength and

power to execute. This actuality is simply because, Satan, the thief

and the prince of this world, ever since he usurped power from

Adam, has set his battle stage to "steal and kill and destroy;" but

Jesus has come that men and women may have life and have it in

fullness (John 10:10). For this reason, *"the Son of God appeared to destroy the devil's work*" (1 John 3:8). Luke adds that Jesus himself was clothed with power when he writes, "*how God anointed Jesus of Nazareth with the Holy Spirit and power, and how he went around doing good and healing all who were under the power of the devil, because God was with him*" (Acts 10:38). The exalted Christ pours out on those he sends the same Spirit who empowered him to carry out his mission.[1]

Again, the primary mission of Christ is the redemption of humanity from the power of Satan, sin, and eternal damnation. Though he is God, but during his days on earth in the flesh, Christ needed to be empowered for the task the Father has given to him. In line with this, it is very glaring in the Gospels that our Lord Jesus Christ never began any major missiological endeavor until he was empowered by the Holy Spirit at the event of his baptism by the river of Jordan through John the Baptist. Luke record has it, ". . . *Jesus was baptized too. And as he was praying, heaven was opened, and the Holy Spirit descended on him in bodily form like a dove. And a voice came . . . from heaven; You are my Son whom I love . .*

---

[1] Michael W. Goheen, *Introducing Christian Mission Today: Scripture, History and Issues* (Downers Grove, IL: IVP Academic, 2014),63.

." (Luke 3:21-22). This really should mean a lot to us as believers, missionaries, teachers of the word and as preachers of the gospel.

In Luke 3:21-22, we read of the baptism of Jesus and how the Holy Spirit came upon him. If John the Baptist was filled with the Holy Spirit from his mother's womb, Jesus was too. He overcame temptation for 30 years through the help of the Holy Spirit. Yet we read here that the Holy Spirit came upon him when he was 30 years old and anointed him for his ministry (Acts 10:38). Poonen maintains that many argue saying that since we are born of the Spirit, there is no need of any further encounter or experience of the Spirit. But Jesus was born of the Spirit too in Mary's womb. He had the Holy Spirit in him for 30 years. Yet he needed to be anointed with the Holy Spirit before he began his ministry.[2] You will recall that just immediately after this phenomenon (his baptism), the ministry of Jesus took a new effective dimension. Back in Mark 1 also, we have two important factors in the Spirit. Jesus was filled with the Holy Spirit; and was driven by the Spirit's power. After Jesus had been clothed with Spirit (cf Acts 10: 38), his witnessing became powerful and impactful anywhere he went. With this

---

[2] Poonen, *Through the Bible: A Message for Today from every Book of the Bible*, 590.

illustration, it can be deductively affirmed that throughout the ministry of Christ on earth; the Holy Spirit was always seen working unanimously with Christ. He never operates without the Spirit (Luke 5:17).

The ministry of the Holy Spirit is mentioned at the beginning of each of the first five books of the New Testament. This reveals to us the tremendous importance of the roles of the Holy Spirit in the New Covenant church. Hence, the ministry of the Holy Spirit remains as one of the foremost things in Christendom that the devil wants to counterfeit today. This accounts for the main reason we see plenty of counterfeit baptisms today. How does the devil ensure that the believers will never get this real baptism? First, by giving some of them a physical or emotional experience. They lack the power to overcome sin and to serve the Lord. But Satan assures them that they have been baptized in the Holy Spirit because they claim to speak some strange languages. Such believers will never again seek the genuine baptism because they are convinced that they have already received it. As I mentioned previously, there are millions of Christians like this everywhere. They are defeated by sin; love money, and live for the world. But they speak gibberish which they called 'tongues' and claim to be getting unusual physical and visual experiences.

Secondly, Satan gets some other believers, who do not believe in manifestations that go with the power of the Holy Spirit, to react against these obvious counterfeits and to stay away from the baptism of the power of the Spirit all together. Hence, Satan succeeds in ensuring that both groups of believers never receive the genuine baptism of power of the Holy Spirit. Do not be satisfied with any cheap or counterfeit baptism; when you genuinely experience this baptism, it will change your whole way of life. The Holy Spirit did not come upon Jesus in power because he is God, but as he came to the world fully man, he lived in obedience to the Father. He was tempted in every way like us, yet he did not sin. The writer of Hebrew writes about him; *"because you loved righteousness, and hated iniquity; therefore, God, even thy God, hath anointed thee with the oil of gladness above thy fellows"* (Heb 1: 9).

If there are still people under the bondage of the devil that need to be set free today, then believers need this power today. No sooner had Jesus begun to preach about the "kingdom" than he began to point his disciples' attention to the reality of spiritual warfare.[3] To begin with, after his comment on the least in the "kingdom" being greater than John the Baptist, Jesus says, *"From the days of John the Baptist until now the kingdom of heaven has suffered violence, and the violent take it by force"* (Matt 11:11-12 ESV). On the first mission trip Jesus sent his disciples, he *"gave them authority to drive out impure spirits and to heal every diseases and sickness"*. When he sent out the seventy, Jesus equally said, '*I have given you authority to trample on snakes and scorpions and to overcome all the power of the enemy . . ."* (Luke 10:19). Jesus also spoke about the imminent invasion of the kingdom of Satan by the kingdom of God: *"I will build my church, and the gates of hades will not overcome it or be able to withstand its assault"* (Matt 16:18). With this awareness, Jesus was establishing the pattern of things to come. His people would be recruited, mobilized, and empowered to move with force against Satan and on behalf of the kingdom of God.[4] There seems to be a cosmic shift in the wielding of power as soon as Jesus completed his mission on earth. Jesus declared, *"All authority in heaven and on earth has been given to*

---

[3] Johannes Verkuyl, *Contemporary Missiology: An Introduction* (Grand Rapids: Eerdmans, 1978), 95. See also, Christopher J. H. Wright, *The Mission of God* (Downers Grove: IVP Academic, 2006), 176-8.

[4] Wagner, *Acts of the Holy Spirit*, 20.

me" (Matt 28:18). After these words, Jesus left the assignment of expanding his kingdom in the hands of people whom the Holy Spirit had empowered for the task. By using their delegated power and authority, they were to declare and manifest the kingdom of God by making disciples of all the nations, baptizing them in the name of the Father and of the Son and of the Holy Spirit.[5] In the next chapter, I will speak on the necessity of the power of the Holy Spirit for effective evangelism.

---

[5] Wagner, *Acts of the Holy Spirit*, 19-20.

Chapter 7

Power for Evangelism

"But you shall receive power when the Holy Spirit
has come upon you; and you shall be witnesses to
Me in Jerusalem, and in all Judea and Samaria,
and to the end of the earth" (Acts 1:8)

Let's see some certain roles of the Holy Spirit in evangelism

that characterized the witnessing of the early church. F. F. Bruce

remarks that in the Gospel of Luke, Luke's description of *"all that*

Jesus began both to do and teach, until the day he was taken up . . .

until the day when, by the Holy Spirit, he commissioned the apostles

whom he had chosen, and charged them to proclaim the gospel

[Acts 1:1-2] exactly summarizes the scope of Luke's Gospel."[1]

Peter Wagner writes, "the Gospel of Luke tells what Jesus did, and

Acts tells what He expects His followers to do both then and now."[2]

This fact vividly portrays the book of Acts as an evangelistic one.

According to Wagner, "Building the Church of Christ, as described

by Jesus and implemented by His followers in the book of Acts,

involves the key elements of both missiology and power

---

[1] F. F. Bruce, *The Book of Acts* (Grand Rapids, MI: Eerdmans, 1988), 30.

[2] C. Peter Wagner, *Acts of the Holy Spirit* (Ventura, CA: Gospel Light, 1982), 17.

ministries."[3] Wagner's point of view here seems to capture well the emphasis of Jesus: *"But you will receive power when the Holy Spirit comes on you; and you will be my witnesses in Jerusalem, and in all Judea and Samaria, and to the ends of the earth"* (Acts 1:8).

From the point of his ascension onward, Jesus meant that the gospel be propagated beyond cultural and geographical boundaries. To this point, Paul Pierson writes,

> These words symbolized the breaking of an almost infinite number of barriers in order that men and women everywhere might hear and respond to the Good News. Just as God in Christ had broken through barriers which separated eternity from time, divinity from humanity, holiness from sin, so His people were broken through geographical, racial, linguistic, religious, cultural and social barriers in order that people of every race and tongue might receive the Good News.[4]

This missiological mandate could not and cannot be implemented by human power alone. Despite the teachings and the expertise on evangelism that the disciples had learned from Jesus in the three years of working and walking with him, Jesus had told them to *"stay in the city* [i.e., Jerusalem] *until you have been clothed with power from on high"* (Luke 24:49). In short, the disciples were not yet fully equipped to face the task ahead of them, they needed the Holy Spirit

---

[3] Wagner, Acts of the Holy Spirit, 18.

[4] Paul E. Pierson, *Themes from Acts* (Ventura, CA: Regal Books, 1982), 11.

this time to be their companion. Today, sometimes, it is easy to get caught up in techniques, methodologies, and resources, especially when they have yielded positive results in the past. The supernatural presence and power of God is highly needed to fulfill God's purpose concerning gospel proclamation.[5]

The Strategic Roles of the Holy Spirit in Evangelism

When the Lord Jesus Christ was going to be with his Father, he gave his disciples a mandate to reach the world with the gospel. However, he was not presumptuous, and believers should not be either; believers cannot afford to jump the gun. He said, *"Wait for the promise of the Father"* (Acts 1:4). Embarking on evangelism without the power of the Holy Spirit is like driving a car without a stirring—it is indeed like getting involved in a fruitless mission. Part of the reasons why there are no productive outcomes among some of the modern-day evangelistic outreaches may be linked to Christians not being spiritually equipped enough.[6] There is a danger of having zeal without knowledge. Believers need to be endowed with the Holy Spirit before they can become effective witnesses. This truth always leaves Christians without the option of whether to

---

[5] Wagner, *Acts of the Holy Spirit*, 50.
[6] Poonen, *Through the Bible: A Message for Today from every Book of the Bible*, 591.

be filled with the Holy Spirit as they present the gospel; it is an absolute requirement to be filled with the Holy Spirit constantly.

From the day of Pentecost onward, dynamism took over the pattern of evangelism by the apostles' specifically, and other believers. The Holy Spirit is the Spirit of missions and is portrayed in Scripture as overseeing missional activities. In this regard, "From the book of Acts we note that the Holy Spirit is the initiator, motivator and superintendent of world missions. All major steps of expansion were divinely initiated and divinely inspired. The Holy Spirit was the Supreme Strategist."[7] At this juncture, it is wise to itemize the role of the Holy Spirit in missions as seen in the entire new Testament era through the apostles and the rest of believers. All that the Holy Spirit does in the book of the Acts (i.e., in the early church) cannot be exhausted in this book.

The Holy Spirit bears witness through believers: One of the prominent roles of the Holy Spirit is to bear witness about Christ.[8] As Jesus said, *"But when the helper comes, whom I will send to you from the Father, the Spirit of truth, who proceeds from*

---

[7] George W. Peters, *A Biblical Theology of Missions* (Chicago: Moody Press, 1972), 229.

[8] Samuel Escobar, *The New Global Mission: The Gospel from Everywhere to Everyone* (Downers Grove, IL: InterVarsity Press, 2003), 124.

the Father, he will bear witness about me. And you also will bear witness" (John 15:26-27). Hence, the Holy Spirit bears witness about Christ to believers, and the Spirit also bears witness through the believers to unbelievers.

Power for witnessing: Really, we are constantly on a stretch, if not on a strain to devise or strategize new methods, new organizations, and better plans in our curiosity to advance the gospel of Christ Jesus. However, we quickly forget as E. M. Bounds said, that; "the Holy Spirit does not flow through method but flows through men, neither does he come on machinery but on men. More so, God does not anoint plans but men," [9] —men who make themselves available for the Spirit to use for the work of missions or ministries. This current trend of reliance on human strength can easily make us forget and neglect the unfathomable roles of the Holy Spirit in our respective ministries and callings, this can makes us depend on a self-mechanized system of converting sinners and in doing missions. In some evangelistic endeavors of many mission bodies, church agents and individuals; the impact of the Holy Spirit is directly or indirectly removed, as major emphasis for the

---

[9] E. M. Bounds, *Power Through Prayer* (Hobesound: Gospel Publication Mission, 2000), pp. 7-8

78

proclamation of the gospel centers on money and human powers. There is tendency to forget that the backbone of all missional and spiritual activities lies on the enablement of the 'Spirit' of Christ. The good news is that Jesus Christ was crucified for our sins and raised from the dead for our justification (Rom 4:25). Similar to the definition of the gospel I gave in chapter one, Bruce Ware summarizes the gospel as follows:

> Christ died for our sins in accordance with the Scriptures, that he was buried, that he was raised on the third day in accordance with the Scriptures, and that he appeared . . . (1 Cor 15:3-5a). According to Paul, "*if you confess with your mouth that Jesus is Lord and believe in your heart that God raised him from the dead, you will be saved*" (Rom 10:9). The gospel, then, is the good news about Jesus Christ—his sinless life, his substitutionary and atoning death, and his victorious resurrection to newness of life—and that by faith in him, we may be saved.[10]

As simple as this message of the gospel appears, no one should present it with presumption. The Spirit must empower the proclamation. His empowerment accounts for the reason why Jesus commanded the disciples not to begin proclaiming the gospel until they were endowed with power; the Spirit would empower them for the task of witnessing. Ware expresses that "the gospel of Jesus

---

[10] Ware, *Father, Son, and Holy Spirit: Relationships, Roles, and Relevance*, 113.

would go forth as the Spirit of Jesus would empower the proclamation of Jesus."[11] Along the same lines, David Platt writes, "While every Christian wants to experience the power of the Holy Spirit, we often forget that the Spirit's power is given for the purpose of being his [Christ] witnesses. Experiencing God, which is the longing of every true believer, happens when we are being his witnesses and making disciples."[12] The purpose of the Spirit coming upon the disciples was to empower them to bear witness about Christ in Jerusalem and beyond (Acts 1:8). The Spirit indeed gives power to believers so that they can testify effectively to the gospel. In Acts, Luke writes, *"With great power the apostles continued to testify to the resurrection of the Lord Jesus. And God's grace was so powerfully at work in them all"* (Acts 4:33). The Holy Spirit indeed empowers the church for global evangelism.

Boldness for witnessing: Prior to the day of Pentecost, the disciples were afraid of the Jewish leaders. Peter denied knowing Jesus three times, but the same Peter and John confronted the Sanhedrin face to face, saying: *"Judge for yourselves whether it is*

---

[11] Ware, *Father, Son, and Holy Spirit: Relationships, Roles, and Relevance*, 113.

[12] David Platt, *Follow Me: A Call to Die, a Call to Live* (Carol Stream, IL: Tyndale House, 2013), xvi.

right to obey you rather than God" (Acts 4:18-19.). The Sanhedrin could no longer stop them from preaching the gospel. The communal prayer of the early believers centers on boldness to preach the gospel[13]: *"Now, Lord, consider their threats and enable your servants to speak your word with great boldness . . . After they prayed, the place where they were meeting was shaken. And they were filled with the Holy Spirit and spoke the word of God boldly"* (Acts 4:29-31).

Regeneration of lost souls: No missionary, evangelist, or preacher of the gospel, no matter how eloquent he or she may be, has the power to convert sinners. The work of conviction and regeneration is done in the mission field only by the Holy Spirit (John 16:8). Billy Graham, in his life-transforming book on the Holy Spirit, maintains that "in regard to the world, the Spirit's work is twofold. First, He has come to reprove it of sin, righteousness, and judgment . . . His second work in the world is to hinder the growth of lawlessness, that is, to engage in the ministry of preservation . . . (2 Thessalonians 2:7)."[14] The Spirit inspired Peter's

---

[13] Zane Pratt et al., *Introduction to Global Missions* (Nashville, TN: Publishing Group, 2014),98.

[14] Billy Graham, *The Holy Spirit: Activating God's Power in Your Life* (Waco, TX: Word, 1978), 32-33.

message so much that the people listening to him were pricked in their hearts and repented (Acts 2:36-37.). Our major task is to present the gospel in the power of the Holy Spirit and leave the result(s) to God. Harold Cook emphasized this truth by saying, "Membership in the church of Christ is by faith, it is by the operation of the Holy Spirit in the human heart, bringing about man's regeneration or the 'new birth' . . . It is the Holy Spirit who must incline the heart of man to accept the message."[15] More to this, Kane said, "God the Father purposed and designed the plan of salvation; God the Son procured and assumed the plan of salvation; God the Holy Spirit executes and administers the plan of salvation."[16]

The Holy Spirit works miracles during witnessing: The Holy Spirit performed many miraculous signs and wonders through the hands of the apostles (Acts 5:12). The Spirit, both in the past and still in the present, confirms the message of the gospel with miraculous manifestations. The book of Acts is filled with signs and wonders wrought by believers. It does not matter what view one

---

[15] Harold R. Cook, *An Introduction to Christian Missions* (Chicago: Moody Press, 1971), 222.

[16] J. Herbert Kane, *Christian Missions in Biblical Perspective* (Grand Rapids: Baker Book House, 1976),303.

holds today; cessationist or continuationist, the truth is, miracles still happen in mission field, and within the body of Christ, today through the Spirit of God and as God chooses.[17] The Holy Spirit is the Spirit of miracles, and he will continue to back up the proclamation of the gospel with power, signs and wonders. Reflecting on the movement of the Holy Spirit in the book of Acts, Tennent writes,

> The Holy Spirit extends the inbreaking of the New Creation through the powerful manifestation of signs and wonders and the holiness of life . . . The manifestation of signs and wonders was not limited to the apostles but also was evidenced in the ministry of Stephen (6:8) and Philip (8:6, 13). The signs and wonders were understood to accompany the preaching of the Word to provide divine confirmation of God's presence working through the church, bringing unity of word and deeds.[18]

Nevertheless, caution must be taken because of the multiplicity of fake miracles and fake workers of miracles in Christendom today. Besides, missionaries need not be troubled about whether they have witnessed any physical or visible miracles in their lifetimes. The Holy Spirit works as he wishes and as he

---

[17] Greear, *Gospel: Recovering the Power that Made Christianity Revolutionary*, 162, 169. See also, Reinhard Bonnke, *Evangelism by Fire: Igniting your Passion for the Lost* (Frankfort, Germany: Full Flame, 2003), viii-x

[18] Timothy C. Tennent, *Invitation to World Missions: A Trinitarian Missiology for the Twenty-First Century* (Grand Rapids: Kregel, 2010), 413-14.

deems fit. God knows best regarding where and when to permit miracles for his own glory.[19] Much more importantly, the conversion of a sinner from the kingdom of darkness to the kingdom of light is the greatest miracle in the whole universe.

The Holy Spirit commissions people for missional task: When men were needed for the work of missions, one of the criteria for selection was that they be Spirit-filled (Acts 6:3). The twelve disciples were ordinary laymen of whom the Pharisees and the Sanhedrin said, 'These people are unschooled and unlearned' (Acts 4:13 paraphrased). However, later in Acts, the apostles commissioned Paul and Barnabas for missions by the leading of the Holy Spirit,[20] as Luke writes, *"Now in the church at Antioch there were prophets and teachers: Barnabas, Simeon called Niger, Lucius of Cyrene, Manaen (who had been brought up with Herod the tetrarch) and Saul. While they were worshiping the Lord and fasting, the Holy Spirit said, 'Set apart for me Barnabas and Saul*

---

[19] The Normative of miracles for today, as witnessed in the early days of the church have come under several arguments as aforementioned. Nevertheless, "When the Holy Spirit comes upon followers of Jesus Christ, the most unlikely people become the fountains of power. This spiritual power is always available, and he displays it according to his sovereign plan. God imparts his power when and how he wants to." See Hughes, *Acts: The Church Afire*, 19.

[20] Pratt et al., *Introduction to Global Missions*, 100-101.

for the work to which I have called them'" (Acts 13:1-2). A. J. Gordon opined that "the Holy Spirit calls out missionary witnesses; and when he calls, his chosen ones will hear, even though a dead church and secular clergy have no notification of their appointment."[21] Perhaps, one of the reasons why there is so much tension today in churches and missions is that men and women are, in some places, chosen for God's works based on their academic qualifications, financial capacities, positions in the society and the likes. They are not chosen based on the criterion of "being filled with the Holy Spirit."

Guidance in missions: On the guiding role of the Spirit, Kane says that "the Holy Spirit is the executive Director [of Mission] here on earth." [22] The Spirit directs believers and missionaries to places where he sees the needs for the fully ready harvest. He redirected Paul to Macedonia contrary to where Paul was heading. Luke the historian has this in his report: *When they came to the border of Mysia, they tried to enter Bithynia, but the Spirit of Jesus would not allow them to. So they passed by Mysia and went down to Troas. During the night Paul had a vision of a*

---

[21] A. J. Gordon, *The Holy Spirit in Missions* (Harrisburg, PA: Christian, 1968), 62.

[22] Kane, *Christian Missions in Biblical Perspective*, 131.

man of Macedonia standing and begging him, 'Come over to Macedonia and help us.' After Paul had seen the vision, we got ready at once to leave for Macedonia, concluding that God had called us to preach the gospel to them. (Acts 16:7-10).[23] When missionaries are controlled by flesh, emotion and empty zeal, they easily fall into the error of going into wrong places at the wrong time, where the fruit is not ripe for harvest. This kind of activity always leads to rejection, discouragement, failure and a departure from the mission field.

The Spirit resolves tensions and conflicts among the witnessing team. The ethnic divisions and tensions in Acts 6 were subsided by the help of the Holy Spirit. He is the Spirit of unity who unites Christ's body and mission-workers. The Scriptures affirm the joint decision of the apostles when they said; *"Brothers and sisters, choose seven men from among you who are known to be full of the Spirit and wisdom"* (Acts 6:3 NIV). The apostles Paul and Barnabas,

---

[23] Paul and his friends were kept by the Holy Spirit from preaching the word in the province of Asia. And then, one night, God guided Paul and his colleagues into a vital new direction through the dream of the man of Macedonia, calling for help. The entire European orientation of the gospel sprang from that incident. The church in Ethiopia was founded as a result of the Spirit nudging Philip to draw alongside a strange man who was reading the scriptures alone in his chariot as he traveled on desert road. See Green, *30 Years that change the World: A Fresh Look at the Book of Acts,* 265.

who were co-workers once, had such a sharp disagreement on one of their mission trips. But instead of this conflict impeding the spread of the gospel, it only served as an impetus and catalyst that sped up the advancement of the gospel to various places under the Roman Empire.[24] No wonder that Oswald J Sander maintains, "Spiritual leadership requires Spirit-filled people. Other qualities are important; to be Spirit-filled is indispensable."[25] Of course, Paul and Barnabas eventually reunited and re-strategized (1 Cor 9:6). Again, the issue of cultural issues and divisions surfaced in Acts 15.[26] However, with the help of the Holy Spirit, the problem was resolved amicably. J. E. Adams once writes,

> When we not only plan, but also submit our plans to the Spirit for His blue-penciling, we do well. We must remember that all the scriptures say about the necessity for good leadership was inspired by the Holy Spirit Himself. Leadership, planning, and management are not merely tolerated or permitted, but required and encouraged by the Holy Spirit. To put it tersely, biblical Administration is spiritual.[27]

---

[24] Danny McCain, *Tough Tests for Top Leaders: God's Strategy for Preparing Africans to lead Global Christianity* (Jos, Nigeria: Moore Books, 2005), 53-5.

[25] Oswald J. Sanders, *Spiritual Leadership* (India: Oasis International, 1967), 79.

[26] Barje S. Maigadi, *Divisive Ethnicity in the Church in Africa* (Kaduna, Nigeria: Baraka Press, 2006), 206.

[27] J. E. Adams, *Shepherding the God's Flock* (Grand Rapids: Zondervan, 1975), 317.

Hence, the apostles' resolution ended with these words: "It seemed good to the Holy Spirit and to us not to burden you with anything beyond the following requirements . . ." (Acts 15:28 NIV).

The Spirit gives spiritual gifts for the edification of Christ's body: One of the ways the Spirit strengthens gospel's presentation is by giving spiritual gifts to the church for the purpose of edification (1 Cor 12:7-11). It is not an overstatement to suggest that there can barely be any success in the church's witnessing when these spiritual endowments are absent. Peters, again on his keen observation on the day of Pentecost, opined that "the Holy Spirit came to qualify those whom God calls out for his ministry by bestowing special gifts (Charismata) upon them"[28], and also upon all believers as they go about testifying to the gospel of Jesus Christ.

The Spirit gives passion, compassion and a burden for evangelism: The burden and passion to evangelize comes from the Spirit. In Acts 6, the apostles resolved to choose men who would be in charge of the table (welfarism), but they said of themselves, "*We will turn the responsibility over to them and will give ourselves to prayer and the ministry of the word*" (Acts 6: 3b-4). The phrase "ministry of the word" is the spreading of the good news and the

---

[28] Peters, *A Biblical Theology of Missions*, 299.

teaching of the Word of God. Christians cannot be filled with the Holy Spirit and not also carry a burden in their hearts for and be passionate about lost souls.[29] The Apostle Paul was so burdened for the salvation of his fellow Israelites. He expressed his passionate desire for them to be saved when he said, *"Brothers and sisters, my heart's desire and prayer to God for the Israelites is that they may be saved. For I can testify about them that they are zealous for God, but their zeal is not based on knowledge"* (Rom 10:1-2). Right from the beginning of the letter to the Romans, Paul made his burden for the gospel known: "I am a debtor to the gospel; I am eager to preach the gospel; I am not ashamed of the gospel" (Rom 1:14-16 paraphrased).

After the outpouring of the power of the Holy Spirit upon the early believers, they spread out to reach almost every area within the Roman Empire,[30] in an age when there was no social media as means of communication. Again, the reason for such widespread missions is that all the early Christians saw themselves as witnesses; there was no idea of 'let the generals fight the war.' Frankly

---

[29] One of the reasons for the spiritual gifts as Green emphasizes is for the purpose of showing compassion for those who are in need both physical and spiritually. See Green, *30 Years that change the World: A Fresh Look at the Book of Acts*, 264.

[30] Pratt et al., *Introduction to Global Missions*, 101.

speaking, laypeople are the key to the evangelization of the world[31] if they would simply allow the Holy Spirit to use them. Luke expresses it this way: *"Therefore they that were scattered abroad went everywhere preaching the word"* (Acts 8:4 KJV). Today, James Kennedy still observes that "for the vast majority of Christian church members, the idea has firmly taken root in their minds that it is primarily the task of the minister to fight the battles for Christ—especially for the souls of men. In the minds of most, the work of evangelism is the work of professionally trained men."[32]

Protection in the face of danger: The evangelistic mandate is the most difficult of all tasks. Jesus told his disciples that they would be like sheep in the midst of the wolves (see Matt 10:16). Stephen Neil says it best: "Christian missionary work is the most difficult thing in the world. It is surprising that it should ever have been attempted."[33] However, on the day of Pentecost, the disciples received the love, passion, zeal and missionary Spirit, not minding the odds. They all became bold and ever ready to lay down their lives for their conviction about the gospel. The Lord promises to be

---

[31] D. James Kennedy, *Evangelism Explosion* (Wheaton, IL: Tyndale, 1970), 3

[32] Kennedy, *Evangelism Explosion*, 3.

[33] Stephen Neil, *Call to Mission* (Philadelphia: Fortress Press, 1970), 23.

with believers from the beginning to the end. Until the believers' assignments and purposes are fulfilled on earth, God does not allow death to claim their lives.[34] Peter, Paul and others were saved several times from death until they fulfilled their evangelistic mandate.

Victory during power encounters comes through the Spirit: The gospel which many people or teams of people take to different places seems to tend much more toward charity donations. The fact remains that Charity donation is quite different from gospel proclamation.[35] For instance, participating in mercy ministries may help to commend the gospel. Again, displaying God's compassion and kindness reveal fruit bearing life of a Christian. Nevertheless, all these actions are good, but they are not evangelism.[36] The presentation of the true gospel makes missionaries vulnerable to the attack of the cohorts of darkness. Frontier missionaries are, on daily

---

[34] Poonen, *Through the Bible: A Message for Today from every book of the Bible*, 981.

[35] For further reading, John Stott argues well on the balance of social works and evangelism. See, John Stott, *Christian Mission in the Modern World* (Downers Grove, IL: IVP Books, 2008), 41-3

[36] Mark Dever, *The Gospel and Personal Evangelism* (Wheaton, IL: Crossway, 2007), 75. Charles Fielding put it right this way, "All of the social services in the world will never be able to stem the tide of suffering on this earth. Every life that is saved through these expensive services will still end up dying and, without the Gospel, will enter into hell." See, Fielding, *Preach and Heal: A Biblical Model for Missions*, 8.

basis, in a face-to-face battle with Satan, the prince of this world, and his agents. Victory, however, comes through the power of the indwelling Holy Spirit. The Apostle Peter was said to be full of the Holy Spirit and he rebuked Simon the sorcerer (Acts 8). Also full of the Holy Spirit, the Apostle Paul rebuked a Jewish sorcerer and a false prophet named Bar-Jesus (or Elymas). The Scriptures say of this incident,

> *Then Saul, who was also called Paul, filled with the Holy Spirit, looked straight at Elymas and said, "You are a child of the devil and an enemy of everything that is right! You are full of all kinds of deceit and trickery. Will you never stop perverting the right ways of the Lord? Now the hand of the Lord is against you . . ." When the proconsul saw what had happened, he believed, for he was amazed at the teaching about the Lord.* (Acts 13:9-12)

The most significant aspect of this recorded incident was that the proconsul saw the supremacy of the power in the name of Jesus and believed.

The Holy Spirit produces result in evangelism: At times, Christians can be tempted to see results from a human point of view. But, the yardstick for measuring success always falls short of God's standard. That missionary "A" has ten converts and missionary "B" has two converts does not mean that the former is more hardworking and more acceptable before God than the latter. The Holy Spirit crowns all missions' efforts with success, and he alone knows the measure and worth of each person's work.[37] Again, no missionary, preacher, evangelist, or believer has within him- or herself the inherent power to bring about the regeneration of lost souls. The work of regeneration is done by the Holy Spirit alone.[38] This reality is why Christians should not get discouraged when they do not win a convert after they have presented the gospel effectively. As previously mentioned, evangelism is presenting the gospel in the power of the Holy Spirit and leaving the results for God.[39]The only thing God demands from believers is faithfulness in their missional activities. Only God knows what he uses to measure success in evangelistic endeavors. It is best to leave the results up to him.

Progress in the face of persecution: As already noted, the Greek word *martureo* means "to witness." From this word comes the term "martyr." The word martyr also refers to a witness who is ready to die for the message to which he or she testifies. For instance, during the trial for his life, Peter made it known to his

---

[37] Ernest C. Reisinger writes that at the end of all gospel conversation (instantly or latter), "Salvation is one result, and damnation is another result." See Ernest C. Reisinger, *Today's Evangelism: Its Message and Methods* (Philipsburg, NJ: Craig Press, 1982), 11-3.

[38] Stott, *Christian Mission in the Modern World*, 185-6.

[39] J. I Packer, *Evangelism and the Sovereignty of God* (Downers Grove, IL: InterVarsity Press, 2012),41.

persecutor that "*Jesus is the stone that was rejected by you, the builders, which has become the cornerstone. And there is salvation in no one else, for there is no other name under heaven given among men by which we must be saved*" (Acts 4:11-12). This Galilean fisherman who once denied knowing Jesus three times now found courage through the power of the Holy Spirit to make this bold declaration even in when on trial. Peter before the Pentecost failed to find the fortitude to make public his commitment to Christ (Matt 26:69–74). Post-Pentecost Peter stood for his Lord so boldly and sacrificially that he paid for his faith with his life.[40] According to the fourth-century church historian Eusebius of Caesarea, the Apostle Peter was forced to watch his wife's martyrdom, then he was crucified upside down, for he had requested that he might suffer in this way.[41]

The evangelistic task, right from the start of the church, has been characterized by severe persecutions. The Jerusalem church was scattered by persecution (Acts 7-8); yet, the persecution only aided in spreading the gospel wider and farther. Under the Roman

---

[40] See R. Kent Hughes, *Acts: The Church Afire* (Wheaton, IL: Crossway Books, 1996), 42.

[41] Kirsopp Lake, *Eusebius: Ecclesiastical History in Two Volumes I* (Massachusetts: Harvard University Press, 1949), 269.

Empire and its emperors, the church was said to have experienced ten consecutive periods of acute persecution so that it was generally believed that "the blood of the martyrs is the seed of the gospel."[42] To date, the persecution against Christianity is on the increase. Yet, the gospel keeps advancing to different parts of the world, even down to the remotest places on earth. In line with the biblical names and descriptions of the Holy Spirit – teacher, comforter, and counselor (see John 16) – the Spirit indeed is the consoling factor in the face of difficulties. Thus, amid oppositions, brutal persecutions, obstacles, oppressions, rejections, destructive criticisms, the sword and martyrdom, the Holy Spirit helps the saints to persevere. (Acts 20: 22-24).

Victory over sin comes through the Holy Spirit: The Holy Spirit enables believers to live victorious lives over sin (Rom 6:14). As Tennent affirms, "The same Spirit who transforms the unbelieving nations of the world is the one who transforms our hearts, teaching us to say 'no' to sin and to embrace the righteousness of Jesus Christ." [43] The Holy Spirit does not just empower believers for witnessing, serving and evangelism alone;

---

[42] Neil, *Call to Mission*, 24. This statement, "the blood of the martyrs is the seed of the gospel" was famously coined by Tertullian. See, Alvin Reid, *Introduction to Evangelism* (Nashville, TN: Broadman & Holman Publishers, 1998), 53.

[43] Tennent, *Invitation to World Missions*, 414.

he transforms both Christians' inner lives and their external witnessing.

Prayers and intercession: A friend once said that training and scholastic ability cannot replace the role of fervent and effective prayers in evangelism. As a matter of fact, one of the contrasts in the Christian witnessing today compared to the days of early believers can clearly be seen in the way contemporary Christians value prayer. For instance, when early believers prayed for days, and Peter stood up to preach for about few minutes, then they witnessed thousands saved in a day (Acts 2:41). Today, believers pray for a few minutes, preach for several days, and see no one saved.[44] This phenomenon does not mean that God does not answer short prayers, but it does mean that God wants Christians today to be intentional in their prayers and to pray with fervency. The apostle James clearly says that *"the fervent and effective prayer of the righteous is powerful"* (Jas 5:16a KJV). Another prayer meeting was held by early believers in Acts 4. At the end of their prayer, as Luke writes,

> they raised their voices together in prayer to God and said,
> "Sovereign Lord, . . . grant to your servants to continue to
> speak your word with all boldness, while you stretch out

---

[44] Bounds, *Power through Prayer*, 19.

your hand to heal, and signs and wonders are performed through the name of your holy servant Jesus." After they prayed, the place where they were meeting was shaken, and they were filled with the Holy Spirit and continued to speak the word of God with boldness. (Acts 4:24, 29-31)

Hence, the Holy Spirit enables believers to intercede for lost souls effectively. To sum it up, John Stott puts right when he writes, "I wonder if anything is more needed for Christian mission in the modern age than this healthy fusion of humility and humanity in our reliance on the power of Holy Spirit."[45]

In most places today, Christendom so much relies on human efforts in evangelizing the unreached people. It is good to use modern technologies, machineries, methodologies, skills, formal education, and great organizations—but we must never allow them to take the place of the Holy Spirit in evangelistic activities. E. M. Bounds writes, "What the church needs today is not more machinery or better tools, not new organization or more novel methods, but men whom the Holy Spirit can use—men of prayer."[46]

The Spirit empowers believers to suffer Martyrdoms: When we are genuinely empowered by the Spirit, we will come to a point where we will no longer be afraid of dying for the sake of

---

[45] Stott, *Christian Mission in the Modern World*, 191.
[46] E. M. Bounds, *Power through Prayer* (Grand Rapids: Baker Book House, 2000), 8.

the gospel. *"But Stephen, full of the Holy Spirit, looked up to heaven and saw the glory of God, and Jesus standing at the right hand of God. "Look," he said, "I see heaven open and the Son of Man standing at the right hand of God . . . While they were stoning him, Stephen prayed, "Lord Jesus, receive my spirit." Then he fell on his knees and cried out, "Lord, do not hold this sin against them." When he had said this, he fell asleep.* (Acts 7:55-60). I am sure that this scenario of Stephen's death communicated a unique message to Paul.

From the passage of the scriptures above, one, it is a genuine mark of the fullness of the Spirit to die in the hand of the persecutors without denying Christ. Second, it is the highest mark of the baptism of power to pray for the forgiveness of your killer while you are drawing your last breath. Stephen took after Jesus whose last petition to God was to forgive his persecutors. Hence, it is a clear mark of immaturity when Christians engage in raining down curses upon their persecutors. When one of the killers of Jesus saw Jesus' reaction to crucifixion by praying for those who crucified him, he said; definitely, this is the Son of God (Mk 15: 39). In the same way, Paul was there when Stephen was being stoned to death. *"At this they covered their ears and, yelling at the top of their voices; they all rushed at him, dragged him out of the city and began to stone him. Meanwhile, the witnesses laid their coats at the feet of a young man named Saul"* (Acts 7:57-58). I believe that Paul was touched when he saw the way Stephen died without cursing his persecutors. He heard Stephen saying 'Lord forgive them . . .' So, when he saw the great light, and heard the voice calling his name, he too said; who are you Lord? Our reactions to insults, oppositions and persecutions define the level of our immersion in the Holy Spirit. Many of the early martyrs faced death with joy because of their faith in Christ.

To sum up this chapter, "I believe the greatest challenge we face in engaging our fallen culture lies not in the culture but in ourselves. All that Jesus has ever done, he can still do. All of God there is, is in this moment. But he can do through us only what we allow him to do in us through the Holy Spirit. Self-reliance constricts the Holy Spirit. He can use fully those who depend fully on him. His best for us is far better than our best for ourselves."[2]

---

[2] Jim Denison Forum, April 19, 2021

Chapter 8

Counterfeit Baptisms

"You will know them by their fruits. Do men gather grapes from thorn bushes or figs from thistles?"
(Matt 7:16)

Christianity begins to enter another fresh era of darkness when the modern-day Christianity began to measure the anointing of the Holy Spirit (baptism of Power) with sign gifts, material and monetary prosperity (look out for my new Book on, 'Nigerian Neo-Pentecostals: A Glimpse into African Modern Christianity').The first time I travelled from my hometown to live in a big city, as a young boy raised in an evangelical church, I found myself in a compound where my next-door neighbor was a young man who was co-habiting with his girlfriend— Even though they were not married yet lived like they were married. Both were workers in the same church. The same lady engaged me in arguments several times, commenting that my church denomination is a cold denomination because, according to her, we do not believe in the second work of grace with the ability to speak in tongues. Two or three times she engaged me in prayers, and as usual, she would always speak in tongues whenever and anytime we prayed. My worry was, but she spoke in tongue, and to my understanding then, only those who are baptized with the Holy Spirit speak in tongues because they are in a higher level of relationship with the Lord. More so, I have a high regard for Pentecostals brethren, and I do not know that a person can be living in sins and yet still speaks in tongues.

When I knew she was cohabiting sexually with her boyfriend, I began to ask myself, what kind of baptism in the Holy Spirit is this? Eventually, as it was his habit, the boyfriend ended up chasing her out of the house to bring another pretty lady from the church. She left with tears, pain and raining curses upon him. His usual habit was to live with a girl for 6 or 8 months and then send them packing. Yet, they all spoke in tongues. This type of soulish tongue is surely not from the Holy Spirit – it is a counterfeit one! It is a mere noise without substance — a noise without holy life.

In another place, a brother in a church went to visit a fellow brother who was the choir leader of their church. As soon as he stepped by the door, he heard what sounded like some romantic sexual voices and act. He knocked the door, and all of a sudden, he heard the voices of a man and woman suddenly began prayer and speaking in tongues. With mixed feeling, he went and peeped through the window's curtain only to see that the choir leader and a particular sister he himself knew very well in the choir were committing fornication, yet they were speaking in tongues. There are several abusers of grace like these in churches these days.

Speaking in tongues is not the Hallmark of Spirit Baptism

According to the word of Christ in Acts 1:8, 'power' is the hallmark of the fullness of the Holy Spirit in the life of a believer — not speaking in tongues. For us to be able to differentiate between the real and the counterfeit baptism, there is a great need to understand soulish experience (empty emotional display) and the spiritual encounter. The division of the OT tabernacle is a perfect example of the composition of man. Some scholars taught that man is a dipartite being (consisting of soul and body); some are of the opinion that man is a tripartite being (having a spirit, soul and body). I hold to the later view. In the OT, the tabernacle is divided into three main parts: the outer court, the holy place and the Holy of holies. According to 1 Thessalonians 5:23, man is a trinitarian being; *"And the very God of peace sanctify you wholly; and I pray God your whole spirit and soul and body be preserved blameless unto the coming of our Lord Jesus Christ."* Man consists of spirit, soul and body. The body, which is the flesh, is the physical and visible part of man. The soul of man is the place of intellect, emotion and will. But God dwells in the spirit of man, not in the body or in the soul (mind and emotion). In the Old Testament, there was no clear understanding of the difference between the soul and spirit part of man. But in the New Testament, we receive clearer understanding of these divisions. For instance, Hebrews 4:12 reads, *"For the word of God is quick, and powerful, and sharper than any two-edged sword, piercing even to the dividing asunder of soul and spirit, and of the joints and marrow, and is a discerner of the thoughts and intents of the heart."*

The Holy Spirit and the Word of God have revealed this partition between the soul and the spirit of man. The 'will' of man is the door to the spirit. It is like the veil between the most holy place and the Holy of holies of the Old Testament tabernacle. When Jesus died on the Cross, the veil in the Jerusalem Temple that partitioned the most holy place and the Holy of holies divided from top to bottom. Christ had opened the way for us to enter the most holy place—the presence of God. *"Having therefore, brethren, boldness to enter into the holiest by the blood of Jesus, by a new and living way, which he hath consecrated for us, through the veil, that is to say, his flesh . . ."* (Heb 10:19-20). This is why every believer in Jesus Christ today can enter into God's presence. When Jesus' body was broken and his will crushed, the wall of partition between God and man was taken away and man now has free access to God. Again, the scriptures say of Jesus, 'this is my body, which is broken for you' (1 Cor 11:24); *'For I came down from heaven, not to do mine own will, but the will of Him that sent me'* (John 6:38); *Father, if you be willing, remove this cup from me: nevertheless, not my will, but yours be done'* (Luke 22:42). When our will is broken, we have free access into God's presence and live in the Spirit (through our spirit). Otherwise, we are living in the soul—the holy place where our intellect, emotion and will operate. Hence, when a man is genuinely filled of the Holy Spirit, he has no will of his own any longer; he continues to live in the will of God consistently (Rom 8: 14). What is the use of speaking in tongues when you are not doing the will of God?

There are people from other religions that also maneuver and gear up their souls' power to speak in other tongues. An emotional meeting may not necessarily be a spiritual meeting. Because, God may not have been there at all. God does not dwell inside our emotions and intellects; he dwells in our spirit. You can sing emotionally, feel so wonderful in prayer, and speak in tongues, but still doing all of these in the soul—without entering the Holy of

104

holies (the realm of your spirit and the Holy Spirit uniting together). The prophets of Baal were all excited when they prayed for many hours, but there was no fire. The fire came only when Elijah prayed just within few minutes (cf 1 Kings 18). There are lots of excitements in the soul today in churches. Worshippers wake up their emotions, just like locomotive engines; the instrumentalists play the drums loud, and the music and songs are raised to higher tempo (everything is loud and emotional), then people are told to release themselves by releasing their faith to start speaking in tongues. Yet, after the whole grandiose and scenario, these people still go back to their carnal living.

Ultimately, man communes with God in his spirit's realm, where man's spirit and Holy Spirit relates together. Unfortunately, most people live in the soul's realm, not in the spirit. Most of those who speak in tongues are only mumbling something out from their souls, not from the spirit. This is a mere demonstration of some gibberish and not the baptism of the Holy Spirit. Again, this is a clear display of soul power. You can produce something from your mind (soul) and then call it speaking in tongue (or baptism of the holy Spirit) and yet remain unspiritual. No doubt, there are genuine speaking in tongues. But if you speak in tongues in church on

Sunday morning, then come home in the noon, and with your mother tongue you scream and shout at your spouse, curse or insult people; you are only living in the delusion of counterfeit baptism of the Holy Spirit. What is the use of speaking in tongues when you cannot control your tongue? If you have truly received this baptism of power, one of the evidences is that, the Spirit first of all lays hold of you to control your tongue (James 2). Again, there are Christians who use speaking in tongues as weapon to curse their neighbors or their enemies. This practice is aberrant from biblical Christianity (Matt 5: 44; Romans 12:14; 1 Pet 3:9).

Baptism from Another 'spirit'

Going home from a college after the end of a semester, I boarded a bus with a young lady sometimes ago. Right inside the bus, just before we took off, she fought with two people as a result of impatience. However, about five minutes when we were on our way, she motioned to all the passengers that we needed to pray. She started praying and speaking in tongues loud for some minutes. After the prayer, she started preaching to people to give their lives to Christ. Someone was bold enough to tell her that she is the first person that needed to be born again. Another Christian brother told her to work on her emotions and attitude. Again, her old Adamic nature came alive as she started raining harsh words. She asked the brother, "Who are you to judge me"? One of the challenges in the churches today is that we have so many people in the church who claim to be Christians but whose lives do not in any way resemble that of Christ or any of the New Testament believers. I once confronted a chorister who would always come to church to play instrument on Sunday drunk. His response was that faith is of the heart, and he had supporters in the church who would say, 'do not judge.' People always forget that, most a time, what we do is a reflection of whom we are within. By their fruit we shall know them, says the Scripture (Matt 7:15-20).

You cannot have the Holy Spirit in you and perpetually continue to do unholy things. David Platt once said, "People who claim to be Christians while their lives look no different from the rest of the world are clearly not Christians."[1] Baptism in the 'Holy Spirit' to an average Pentecostal is that you have been filled in the Spirit with an evidence to be able to speak in tongue as Christian. I have countless number of instances of people who I know very well with these kinds of questionable lifestyles (like the one cited above)

---

[1] David Platt, *A Call to Die. A Call to Live: Follow me*, 18.

yet claimed to be baptized in the 'Holy Ghost' just because they murmur some gibberish words called speaking in tongue. Such people are under the control of another spirit, not the Spirit of Christ. Even people of other religion know how to arouse their soulish emotions to speak in other languages (tongues) too. I have seen Muslims and Hindis speaking in tongues. This is why we need discernment to test all the spirits (1 John 4:1). Jesus clearly told us; *"Not everyone who says to me, 'Lord, Lord,' will enter the kingdom of heaven, but only the one who does the will of my Father who is in heaven"* (Matt 7:21).

What about prophets, pastors, evangelists, miracle workers of today with a claim on baptism of the Holy Spirit because they display some certain questionable giftings? There are many fake ministers of the gospel who are deceiving people to believe that they have the power of the 'Holy Spirit.' You can quickly know this by their attitude to money, opposite sex, material things and display of ego. You can't be a lover of money if you are truly under the power of the Holy Spirit. Gehazi was exposed for his love for money and material things (1Kgs 5). The fake conversion of Simon came to limelight when he wanted to buy the gift of the Spirit so that he could add to his magical power and make more gain and popularity in it (Acts 8:18-24). The spirit of mammon can display some acrobatic gimmicks as long as there is going to be a material or monetary reward after the show.

The truth remains that some are called into the ministry today by their own stomach; some because of their desire for fame and popularity. However, we still have the category of those who are genuinely called by God. It is good to also mention that some started well, but along the way, they have been polluted by mammon. You clearly remember that Satan promised to give Jesus a fame, power and the glory of this world if only Jesus would bow to him (Matt 4:1-7). There are many today, who have gotten this fame, they have the power and the riches of this world, but of course, they have bowed to the devil. Hence, not everywhere you see displaying power is really displaying the power of the Holy Spirit. They received their power from the unclean spirits. The amazing mystery of these fake men in ministry is the patience of God, but certainly, a disappointing end awaits such preachers except they repent. To this, Jesus said; *"Many will say to me on that day, 'Lord, Lord, did we not prophesy in your name and in your name drive out demons and in your name perform many miracles?' Then*

I will tell them plainly, 'I never knew you. Away from me, you evildoers!'" (Matt. 7:22-23).

Jesus warned us to "*watch out for false prophets. They come to you in sheep's clothing, but inwardly they are ferocious wolves'* (Matt 7:15). There are myriad of stories of many so called 'men of God' in different countries, who sexually assault members, and who have become extremely rich by exploiting gullible minds and are merchandizing the gospel. Some are caught with diabolical powers; some have become untouchable and risen to the level of deified principalities. It doesn't matter even if souls are being saved under their ministrations, they are neither of God nor are they from God. God was at a point not pleased with Moses and Aaron, yet God brought out water from the rock for His people to drink through Moses and Aaron. Even when the life of Samson was not pleasing to God because of his inordinate affections for strange women, God still used him in power. For more than twelve years, king Saul was still reigning as king over Israel when another king (David) had already been anointed to replace him. These derailed men of God need to return to God in genuine repentance to avoid hearing the voice of God in the Last Day saying, 'I never knew you. Away from me, you evildoers!'

Material Prosperity is not the Hallmark of Power Baptism

We must know that there is a pervasive but wrong definition of biblical prosperity. In Matt 4:17 John said, *"Repent for the kingdom of heaven is near"*. Israel has spent 1500 years from the time of Moses to John the Baptist seeking the things of the earth. They were occupied with the things of the earth. Their blessings were earthly—many children, plenty livestock, victory over earthly enemies, inheriting plenty land, good farm produce, etc. You see more of these as you read the OT. There are not many references to heaven and hell in OT. In Deuteronomy 28 for instance, we read God telling them: if you obey me, I will give you a lot of money, I will give you healthy children—you will not have miscarriages, your cattle will abound in plenty, your storage will overflow, your crops will yield a hundred-fold increase and you will become very rich if only you obey me. Their curses were also earthly. In the same Deuteronomy 28, God says; but if you do not obey me (God did not even say they will go to hell), you would become sick, blind etc. If they continue to disobey God, they were not threatened with Hell but they will not get rain, their crops would wither, their enemies would overpower them and so on.

So, for 1500 years (from Moses to John the Baptist), their minds were set on things of the earth. Hence, they wanted to obey God because of earthly prosperity and physical health. This is a gospel, but it is an Old Covenant gospel. Jesus came with the New Covenant gospel, and it is very interesting how the devil has led the whole Christian preachers all the way back to that Old Covenant gospel again. Today preachers are teaching that if God blesses you, you will be rich in monetary and material things. They teach that if God blesses you, you will live in sound physical health. But we know that all these teachings could not be the truth because other religions teach that—it is not only in Christianity. You go to Muslim countries, and some Muslim will say, "Allah is the true 'God' because he has given us all the oil and all the countries of the world come to us begging for oil because Allah has blessed us. From every country, they come here, and they must please us in the Arab land; all their political policies are determined whether it will please the Arabs, because Allah is the true God. Observe the sheikhs of Saudi Arabia and other countries for instance, they are extremely wealthy and healthy and believe that Allah has blessed them with prosperity.

You go to the Hindus; the Hindu businessmen of India are part of the wealthiest people on earth. They worship the goddess of wealth called 'Lakshmi' the consort of the god Vishnu. These men say Lakshmi is the true 'God' because he makes them wealthy. Again, you listen to modern Christian preachers, and they say, Jesus is the true God because he makes us wealthy. Hence, there is now a great competition between Allah, Lakshmi and Jesus to make people wealthy. If this is now the mark of blessing, I would rather say that Allah and Lakshmi win. Because on a global scale, Muslims and Hindus are richer than Christians. Now you can see the stupidity and the folly of using material wealth as the mark of God's blessing. What about health? Do you think that the healthiest people in the world are Christians? No. If you look at the Guinness Book of Records, people who lived longest are in Afghanistan, Japan and in all the Soviet states. These people worship other gods—they are not Christians. Wealth and health are not the true marks of God's blessings today. And because most Christians have not understood the simple truth of the gospel, they are jumping from one church to another seeking for money and health.[2]

Some think that increases in salary, offer of better job and booming businesses are all hallmark of God's blessing because God is pleased with them. It is so unfortunate how people still carry the

_____

[2] Poonen message on "Basic Christian's Living."

Old Covenant gospel and lift it higher than the true gospel of Christ. I'm not saying God cannot or He is not blessing believers with wealth and good health, but *the unmistaken mark of genuine blessing from God is to become more and more like Jesus Christ.* Even many Christians testify saying 'God has really blessed our children;' not because these children are becoming more like Jesus in their characters, but because they get good jobs in banks, in oil companies, in government parastatals or they travel abroad. This redefinition of true riches and blessings from Christ has plagued Christianity today. If you are still living with this mentality or mindset, then you have not repented from the kingdom of earth and understand that the kingdom of heaven has come which is not a matter of eating and drinking; it is of righteousness, peace and joy in the Holy Ghost (Rom 14:17). This misconception is the real reason why the experience of the Holy Spirit that many Christians claim to have is so shallow and fake. No doubt, God is still blessing his people with material things, but it is never a yardstick for spirituality.

Do you think you have the same baptism in the Holy Spirit that Peter, James, and John got on the day of Pentecost—you who love money, and get angry often and lose your temper? And even though you speak in tongues, you still commit some sins in the secret—you lust after opposite sex, you watch pornography; you are gloomy most of the time and lack the peace and joy of the Spirit. Yet you claim to have the baptism of the Holy Spirit because you speak some strange tongues once in a while. Is this the baptism of the Holy Spirit? Far from it—it is a counterfeit. This is surely not the baptism of the Holy Spirit that Jesus and the apostles had. Again, the preparation for the baptism for the Holy Spirit and fire (Matt 3:11f) remains as turning around from facing the things of the earth and concentrate on seeking the things of the kingdom of heaven (Matt 4:17). Else, you will continue to get counterfeit encounters with the Holy Spirit, and the devil keeps you happy with the counterfeit. On the final day, you will be surprised that you have only been deceived in all your days on earth. If you repent completely and genuinely, you will never be deceived—if you turn around completely toward God, your vision will become clearer.

From Pentecost to Prosperity

What people are seeking for today is a painless Pentecost. But there is no such thing as painless Pentecost! Immediately after the Pentecost, the early believers prospered! The question is, what kind of prosperity did they experience? They prospered because they fulfilled God's purpose for their lives. They prospered because they went to jails and suffered martyrdom for the gospel. It was not material prosperity—it was prison, pain, privation and persecution. Many of today material prosperity preachers are liars and dishonest people! They will not do thorough justice to the biblical interpretations. I am afraid the way preachers are accumulating money and material things for themselves here on earth (where moths destroy) in the name of the anointing. There are many rich Christians that will enter heaven with bankruptcy, whereas some Christians (even though poor on earth) will be super wealthy when they get to Heaven! (James 2:5; Rev 2:9).

Today, men who have turned their acclaimed Pentecost encounter or baptism of the Holy Spirit as a means of financial gains are really not working for God but for themselves—for their stomachs, pockets, ego, self-indulgence and lusts. Their god is their bellies (Philip 3: 18-19; Rom 16: 16-18). For example, it cost time and money Paul to write letters and epistles to the churches, send those writings and never taxed or charged the churches for money. Under the power of the Holy Spirit, the shadow of Apostle Peter healed the sick. Handkerchiefs and aprons from the Apostle Paul healed the sick (Acts 19:12). He never turned this to 'anointed mantle' for sale. The early apostles had several opportunities to make themselves rich through the gospel, yet they never exploited the people of God. If you were privileged to ask the early apostles what true prosperity is, I am much convinced that many of them will tell you that kingdom prosperity is not an accumulation of cars, money in the banks, land and material possessions of any form. Prosperity to them is to become more and more like Jesus daily and to the point of becoming more like Jesus in his death. Therefore, many of them counted it all joy in whatever suffering that came their ways as they followed Jesus Christ. Many of them counted themselves unworthy to die exactly like Jesus Christ. To this, seeing it as the greatest honor, the Apostle Peter requested from his persecutors not to kill him exactly on the cross the way Jesus was crucified. Why did Peter make this request? He told his executioners, "I am not worthy to be crucified like my Lord. Then, having reversed the cross, they nailed his feet up."[3]

Many of these martyrs as they were dying for the sake of the gospel had joy; and were excited for being persecuted for the gospel. When Peter and John were beaten at the public square for

---

[3] *Acts of the Holy Apostles Peter and Paul*, Ante-Nicene Fathers 8.484).

propagating the gospel, as they united back with other fellow believers; they were happy for being persecuted like Jesus Christ (Acts 4). They considered this suffering with Christ as the greatest prosperity. When many of them were dying either on a stake with fire, dying by beheading or being fed to the hungry beasts; they were all dying rejoicing. Not because they have landed property which their children would inherit. The Christianity of today that defines material and monetary accumulations as a mark of prosperity in Christendom is completely a different 'Christianity' with a different 'gospel.'

Then, am I against God's blessings? Absolutely No! God can bless you with cars, money, land houses; but this is not the measurement for prosperity in the kingdom. The focus in the new covenant is the prosperity of the soul through deliverance from sin in the name of Jesus Christ by his atoning sacrifice on the cross. The true prosperity again is becoming more and more like Jesus every day. If you want to disbelieve what I am saying, think about the unbelievers who do not know Jesus Christ, yet they have landed property, rich in money, have expensive cars, houses, possess private jets, with good health, even though they never know Jesus. Do you think this group of people is enjoying prosperity? The materials things that will never go beyond this terrestrial planet-earth? No one can know the true definition of prosperity until he encounters Jesus Christ. And no one is prosperous, no matter the amount of wealth accumulation if he or she is not becoming more and more like Jesus on daily basis. And a man is prosperous or is living in prosperity if he gets his wealth in a godly way and uses his earthly possession for the advancement of God kingdom on earth. This is the true riches and wealth in the kingdom of God. Again, the true riches are prosperity that cannot be quantified by money or material possessions. I urge you to go for the best in Christ, go for the ultimate riches; do not be deceived by the revival of the pseudo-gospel among today's modern churches. The word of God says, he that must boast should boast in this that he knows God (Jer 9: 24; 1 Cor 1: 31; 9:31; 2 Cor 10: 17; Gal 6:14). Boasting on the accumulation of material riches on earth is an empty boast.

Chapter 9

Experiences on the Filling of the Holy Spirit

"Whoever believes in me, as Scripture has said,
rivers of living water will flow from within them"
(John 7:38)

In this chapter, beginning from my personal experience, I will cite some personal encounters of certain individuals on how they got in touch with the infilling of the Holy Spirit. I am struggling not to argue for "baptism in the Holy Spirit as the second work of grace" as postulated by some. But along the line of our conversion, every one of us must come to a certain remarkable point of our relationship with the Holy Spirit. I must be sincere; it is not easy to explain this encounter to anyone except you have gotten there. Again, either you support those who hold onto the second work of grace or infilling of the Holy Spirit or baptism of power etc., my main emphasis in this book is that we all need to encounter the power of the Holy Spirit. Regardless of what stage of your life this power comes in; something is very sure, and that is, you will surely know you get it. Experiences with this power vary, and of course, you and I know that we cannot force our experiences into the Scripture so as not to fall into the error of 'Experiential Theology.' But always remember that the Holy Spirit cannot be caged neither

120

can we fully understand his way in totality. He does as he wills. Baptism into the body of Christ which the Holy Spirit does for everyone at the point of conversion is different from the baptism of power which the Holy Spirit does to prepare everyone for victorious Christian living and for effective services for the advancement of the kingdom of God. In John 20:22, Christ breathed upon his disciples and told them to receive the Spirit. Either we know it or not, something really happened to the disciples at this point. Some believe that this moment was the point of their regeneration as Jesus taught in John 3:1-8 (there is no space for me to go deep into the various arguments on this). But after this, Jesus told them to wait for the power that will come upon them when they would be immersed in the Spirit.

Permit me to say it clearly that we cannot use personal experience to build church doctrinal dogma nor build theology. A true church must build her doctrines on the solid foundation of God's infallible and unchangeable word. However, God still uses different encounters or experiences to draw people closer to Himself or as means to reveal Himself to individuals. It is very appalling when you see fellow Christians discrediting the experience or the encounter of other Christians just because they were not present at the scenes, or because they themselves have not experience the exact thing in their lives. When one talks about the move of the Holy Spirit that he has witnessed, I have heard people saying words like: "yes, we have heard those stories happening in places like South America, Asia, Africa . . . , but how are we sure they are true?" "They may just be mere superstitions of some sorts." The encounters in the Book of Acts are written as witnesses for us today. Let's imagine if the believers in those days termed the miraculous displays that happened through Peter, John and others (including the shadow of Peter healing the sick) as mere superstitions; if the believers of those days denied the experiences and encounters of Philip in Samaria (such as disappearing and reappearing in another geographical location without boarding a plane or automobile car, including some signs and wonders that the Holy Spirit wrought through him); if believers in Jerusalem disbelieved Paul raising Eutychus who fell from the upstairs room building, who was dead already (Acts 20: 7-12), then we wouldn't have a complete book of the Acts of Apostles.

I still have this question to ask; "Is Jesus the Great I am or the Great I was"? If Christ is the 'Great I was,' then, we may not expect any single miracle, sign or wonder today. But if Christ is the same yesterday, today and forever (Heb 13: 8), if what the Apostle John says of Christ, 'I am alive' (Rev 1:18) is real, then, limiting the supernatural move of God to certain age or period of history is irrelevant. Much more, part of the purposes or reasons of this power is to *"do good and set free those who are under the oppressions of Satan"* (Acts 10:38). Doing good here included the spreading of the good news of the liberating power in the Gospel. Again, if there are still people under the oppression of Satan that need to be set free, then, we surely need this baptism of power today. Even though the Book of Acts was written during a unique time in history, certain qualities should always be true of Christians and the church [1] everywhere and anytime. As I delve into some of these experiences from individuals, I want to say emphatically that the infilling of the Holy Spirit is not just a one-time-experience; it is a continuous encounter.

My Personal Encounter

It was in a mid-year conference of my church denomination, Evangelical Church Winning All (ECWA), during the youth wing breakout section in 1994 that I had an encounter with Christ. After

---

[1] David Platt, *A Call to Die. A Call to Live: Follow Me* (Carol Stream: Illinois; Tyndale House Publishes, 2013), ix.

hearing a message on John 3:3, *"Except a man be born again,"* salvation became a thing of personal decision for me. I yielded my life to Christ and since then began a personal relationship with him. All this time, I knew within me that I love the Lord and I was actively committed in my local church. However, I struggled daily with sins (inward lust of all form within me). I was not going around sinning, but deep within me, as a young boy then, I was still burning with passionate lusts that were difficult for me to share with anyone. I lacked boldness in witnessing to sinner about Christ as often as I should be doing.

In the year 1996/97, I came in contact with friends from about four different Pentecostal denominations who told me that I needed a 'second experience,' *"the baptism in the Holy Spirit,"* with the ability to speak in tongues, which is the 'second work of grace.' For a few reasons, I was skeptical about these friends. Even though they claimed to be baptized in the 'Holy Ghost,' I never saw in most of them real fruit of salvation. They honored their Pentecostal leaders but had no regard for their parents. They live ascetic life and looked unhappy every time. Again, among the tongue-speaking believers around me then, I saw in their midst a lot of empty emotionalism, they love money, the men lust after the women; they love to be hailed and making people bow before them. They saw themselves as holy above everyone and tagged all others who were not member of their churches as sinners and mere religious people. They engaged in evangelism with judgmental and condemnation dispositions. They were highly irascible—easily get irritated, touchy, and full of anger. They were also very selfish. I'm sorry, the descriptions above look odd, but I lived with them for about seven years to have known them so well. All these attitudes are opposite of what I lived for. The question within me then was "What form of baptism in the Holy Ghost is this"? Couple with this was the fact that I am a son to a pastor of a well-known evangelical denomination and my denomination stood in opposition then to most of what the Pentecostals stood for. The line of demarcation between evangelicals and the Pentecostals was so sharp that many families of the evangelical have been divided whenever anyone cross over from evangelical to Pentecostals or brought some of the practices of the Pentecostals into evangelical homes. Similarly, if you left Pentecostal for evangelical, you are tagged as a backslider.

In the year 1998, leaving my family, I traveled to college to further my education. The well-known Student Fellowship on my campus then was Nigeria Fellowship of Evangelical Student

(NIFES). Again, I joined this fellowship group and became active, serving the Lord as I enrolled in the choir. To my surprise, NIFES comprises students from different denominational backgrounds. Some are from evangelical, some from Pentecostals, some from Charismatic movement and other denominations. The amazing thing I noticed was that it was a form of unity in diversities. We were one family without any discrimination. The fellow Pentecostals students I met there were friendly, full of joy and were willing to share with others. At this point, I began to open my heart little by little to learn more from other Christians. Several impacting teaching programs were organized by this fellowship every time the school was in session.

Sometimes in the mid of 1998, we held a revival in the school. A charismatic man was invited for three days' revival program. On the last day, he made an altar call for anyone who wants to receive the baptism of the Holy Spirit with ability to speak in tongues. Again, my heart began the usual agitations, questions and doubts. The guest speaker and few brothers were in the front line to lay hands on people. I heard people murmuring some words as hands were laid on them and our Pentecostal guest kept on encouraging them to speak out whatever comes to their mouths.

Words of encouragement were given to those who did not receive the tongue-gift and they were encouraged to release their faith to receive it. Nothing was forthcoming out of me. Several questions and agitations were running through my mind as I went back to my dorm that night.

A Memorable Night

One night before the semester was over; I went on my knees before God and it seemed I received extra ordinary strength as I prayed for about an hour on my knees (for the first time). I told God to let me know if this gift of tongue is still real for today's believers in Christ. That night, I had an encounter I can never forget. In my sleep, I saw myself on a farm working with my father. Suddenly, a terrible and fearful looking man (like a demon) started pursuing me with machete (cutlass). I screamed as I beckoned on my father for help. Unfortunately, when my Dad saw the man, he took to his heels and raced off. This ghost-looking being was getting closer to me with full force and anger. Knowing there was no way out for me, I started praying. The next thing that I saw praying in an unknown tongue. The ghost commanded me to shut up my mouth, but I kept praying out louder. The next thing I saw was that this demonic spirit fell down and started screaming as he was shouting 'Fire! Fire!! Fire

. . !!!!!' He looked like he was under a sulphuric or a brimstone fire. Then, I woke up sweating profusely on my bed. Interestingly, for about two minutes or more, I couldn't stop the praying in tongues. After this encounter, for a complete three days, it was from one revelation to another as I kept seeking God in prayer and fasting. I noticed from then till now, the boldness to witness and compassions for the lost engulfed me. All my lustful desires were gone. At this point, the love for Christ consumed me so much that there is nothing in life that matters to me than doing His will and fulfilling his purpose for my life. I realize the unfathomable depth of his love for me, and now the love for Him overshadowed my previous lustful desires so much that I would not want anything to come in between me and Christ. Right from there in the college, I started witnessing to people that came my way, including a Muslim guy in my hostel who had a terrifying looking beard. Several people there on campus nicknamed me 'Pastor Sam.'

After this encounter, we had a two-week holiday from the college. I tried as much as possible to hide my spiritual fervor from my parents, but it became noticeable. For the purpose of fasting, I skipped meals, I prayed a lot than it used to be, and the Scripture became my companion as I read and meditated time to time. I noticed that the Scripture came alive in me in a way I have never experienced before. But at the same time, I was the family workaholic (as usual). My Mom kept noticing me. She knew in herself that her son was a different person. One day, I was praying in my room, I never knew I had spent two hours on my knees, and 'this tongue of a thing' came into the midst of my prayer. My Mom came to knock at my door and warned of the consequence of praying like the Pentecostals as an evangelical boy. She did not want my father to be labeled as an evangelical pastor who could not control his family. I remember then that some evangelical youths were either put under church discipline or sent away for speaking in tongues. Not to disregard my parents, I spent much of my time going to solitary places in the bush, farm or riversides to pray.

She was set free from demonic sexual bondage

I had been asking God in my personal prayer about the reality of His power to set the captives free as I read in the pages of the New Testament. One of our young adult sisters in my Dad's church was sick. She got sick too often. One of the youth leaders invited me to go together with him so that we can pray with her. She narrated her ordeal that a strange being used to come and have sexual intercourse with her in her dream fortnightly. She would wake from the dream and see herself literally being messed up. The next thing that would follow was for her to get sick for about three to four days. This oppression rendered her hostile, moody, depressed and backward in her studies. We entered the church's prayer room to pray. The brother and I were doing our usual traditional silent prayer until *I heard a strong voice in my human spirit that told me; be bold and lay your hand on her forehead and rebuke the demonic spirit in the name of Jesus.*

After much struggle, I obeyed. Straight on the floor we found her speaking with a manly voice, "She belongs to me; no one can take her away from me." Being the first time I would ever see this, it took us sometime to cast the demon out of her. After about 30 minutes of spiritual warfare, the Lord delivered her completely. Today, she is a happy mother with good home, and she works as a nurse. It was as if God was busy arranging scenario for me to test run the power and the authority in the name of His son, Jesus Christ. After her deliverance, a young pastor invited me to come over to his church to pray for some youths. The same power of God came upon these youths and set them free from all addictions and bondages of darkness. God continued to take me deeper and deeper into the awareness of His power for us who believe in Christ before I ever accepted the call into ministry. I will still cite few examples later. Let me make this clarification quickly: I am not in any way trying to make hero out of my personal experience at all. But even though I have seen people with fake demonstrations of tongues and other gifts of the Spirit, I have equally come across genuine ones. Much more, the Holy Spirit knows where your calling is needed and the gifts you need to be effective in your calling. Nevertheless, I have pastored an evangelical church for about ten years now and I never speak in tongue on the pulpit, but whenever I'm alone in my prayer closet, I speak in tongue if I'm lifted by the Spirit with utterances. Much so, no Christian needs speaking in tongues to cast out devils; you only need to exercise the authority you have in Christ.

Other Examples of How People Encounter the Baptism of Power

I have shared my personal encounter on the infilling of the Holy Spirit that produces power. At this point, let us explore the encounter of few believers when they came under this power of the Spirit. Some are with tongues while many are without tongues as well.

Baptism of Power without tongues: I want to start by establishing the truth that elevating speaking in tongues as a hallmark of baptism in the Holy Spirit or a baptism of power has no concrete biblical basis for its propagation as a doctrine. The Apostle Paul right from the time of the early church established the fact that not everyone is gifted with tongues; and no one is authorized to forbid anyone from speaking in tongues as well (1 Cor.12: 29-30;14: 39). The history of the advancement of Christianity reveals several men and women of great spiritual power who went about spreading the gospel with the demonstration of God's power. Let me begin with Jesus Christ himself. Jesus told us in the gospel that believers will speak in tongues. He is not saying that every single believer must speak in tongues, simply because, the scripture cannot contradict itself (see 1 Cor 12:29). Jesus never spoke in tongues, yet no one on earth is as filled with the Holy Spirit like Jesus. The ministry of John the Baptist was fiery and very practical. People were trooping out from various places to meet him in the wilderness. Yet, we never read of John the Baptist performing any sign and wonder nor healing the sick. He was not recorded to have spoken in tongue. Jonathan Edwards in the first half of the 18th century, preached a sermon "Sinners in the Hands of an Angry God." It looked like hell was opening beneath the feet of people hearing his message. We never read much about him speaking in tongues, yet he brought hundreds of sinners to the Lord. Does anyone want to argue that Jonathan

132

Edwards was not baptized with power? David Brainard was an American missionary to the Native Americans whom God used tremendously. Does anyone want to argue that Brainard was not baptized with power?

Tommie Titcome was a Canadian missionary to Yagba land in the early 20th century. The local idol priest served him with poisoned food. Tommie got home (to his tent) with severe stomach pain. At the point of death, he cried out to God who healed him miraculously. This incident made many of the locals to surrender their lives to Jesus. At another time, the chief priest of idol worshipers diabolically sent a cobra snake to Tommie's bed. Before sleeping, Tommie knelt beside his bed to pray. Unknowingly, he put his hand on the cobra's tail on the bed as he was praying. He felt his hand touched something cold that was at the same time moving. Those days, there was no electricity, he put on the local lamp (lantern) and to his amazement saw that it was a cobra. The priest later confessed his plan to kill this missionary with the demonic snake. Tommie never spoke in tongue.[2] In the 1950s, Revd Andrew P. Stirrett, a doctor and a missionary, served Holy Communion to

---

[2] See Sophie de la Haye, *Tread upon the Lion: The Story of Tommie Titcombe* (Ontario, Canada: Sudan Interior Mission, 1973).

the handful of believers (new converts) in Oro Ago land, Nigeria.[3] A man ate and began to cough. He got home; the cough continued and became wield. When the matter was reported to Stirrett, he said it was because the man had sinned before coming to partake of the Holy Communion. The missionary called the man in, and he confessed sleeping with his neighbor's wife. After his confession and genuine repentance, the Lord forgave him, and he was instantly healed. Does anyone want to argue that Tommie and Stirrett were not baptized with power just because they did not speak in tongues?

In the early 1980s, Cen Sharpe was a missionary at the SIM missions' station in Ilorin, Kwara State Nigeria. Revd Bello staged a musical concert where Sharpe was to present the gospel to people at a long tennis court in Challenge Station. Suddenly, the sky became dark with a threat of a heavy rain. Sharpe stood up to pray by saying, "Lord, Cen is your servant; rain is your servant; one servant does not hinder another; let it not rain here until when we are done." To every body's surprise, the rain started pouring heavily on the street opposite the venue (just some few meters away) of the

---

[3] Dr. Andrew P. Stirrett was a medical doctor and one of the missionaries who started the Mission Station in Patigi, Nigeria.

home that was not even mine), without much money and also having a small child to look after. I became very discouraged and started drifting away from the Lord in my mind. I did not do anything wrong externally. I still went to the church- meetings. But I was miserable inside. I knew that God had led me to marry my husband. But I wondered why we were suffering like this. I did not feel like praying or even reading the Bible. In addition, our baby was keeping me awake at night and I was constantly tired.

At this time of utter discouragement, a sister whom I had never met before came to our home. She asked me if we could pray together. I agreed and took her to my bedroom, and we prayed together. The freshness in her prayer challenged me. It made me long for such a <u>freshness in my own life</u>. That sister then suggested that I go to her house next time for prayer. So, the next time, I took my baby and went to her home. We both knelt down on the floor and prayed while my baby was sleeping between us. I prayed saying, "Lord something has happened in my life. At one time I was so close to you, but now I have gone so far away from You. Please have mercy on me and bring me back to You."

Then the Lord began to show me how I had wrong attitudes in my heart against some people. My father and I had become distant concert. After they were done, the rain fell all over the place.[4] Does anyone want to argue that Cen was not baptized with power just because he did not speak in tongues?

What about William Carey? His popular quote remains as "Expect Great thing from God, attempt great thing for Him." Without financial support, he went to the dark corner of India with the gospel in abject poverty. He translated Bibles into several Indian local languages. He opened several missions' stations and cleared the way for other missionaries to penetrate India with the gospel. Does anyone want to argue that Carey was not baptized with power just because he did not speak in tongues? D L Moody was a great evangelist of his time that history will not forget in a moment. He never canvassed for every believer to speak in tongues.

Baptism of Power with Signs Gifts

Sister A Testimony (grafted in with permission): Up until my wedding, I had been very active in God's work in the medical college where I studied, and in the hospital where I worked. But about 2 years after that (in early 1970), I was just sitting at home (a

---

[4] Eld Dr Job A. Adewumi an eye witnessed of the incident narrated the story.

from each other. My husband's parents were very good to me, but I was not happy in their home, because it was not my home. The Lord opened my eyes and showed me that the problem was not with others but with me. So, I started crying and said, "Lord, forgive me. I am such a rotten sinner. Outwardly people think I am good. But I am full of bitterness inside."

Suddenly I felt God touching my heart. I felt like a little child in His arms. He picked me up and my tears stopped. He filled my heart with joy and peace once again. As I started to praise and thank God, *I found myself speaking in a new language*. I was surprised. My church background was 'Brethren' - and I did not believe in the gift of *speaking in tongues.* I wondered what was happening to me. I did not want to be praying in that strange language. So, I started praying in English again. *But it was a struggle now to pray in English. I found it easier to pray in the new language God had given me.* I just poured out my heart to the Lord and praised God in this new language. *I felt in my spirit as if I was no longer on earth.* There was such a great joy and peace in my heart. I came back home and told my husband what had happened. And in the coming days, he saw a real change in my life. A new freshness had come into my life. I felt as if the dry barren desert in my heart had suddenly turned fresh and green! That joy and peace has never left me since that day.

Since then, as a family, we have faced many trials from people who opposed us. But none of those things have ever drawn me away from my relationship with the Lord. After our fourth son was born, I was suddenly struck down with rheumatoid arthritis and had to be in bed almost all the time. Even then the Lord kept my heart full of joy and peace – and after one month *He healed me miraculously.* The Lord started a church in our home in August 1975. After that, we faced a lot of opposition from other Christians. We also struggled to meet our family's needs. But in all those situations, God stood by me and strengthened me and answered prayer. I came to know Him more and more intimately as my Father. God then opened my eyes to the great truths of the New Covenant that He had established in Christ. He showed me that He had given me the power of the Holy Spirit so that I would not live for myself anymore, but only for Him. I saw that God wanted to change me into the likeness of Jesus – and He began to change me slowly. He taught me patience and helped me to overcome my anger and filled my heart with love for people.

From Sister A's testimony, look at some of the underlined salient points that matter when you experience the baptism of power of the Spirit. Know again that this encounter is not just a one day or a one moment encounter; it is a continuous phenomenon.

Peace's Encounter: Peace is my wife. In the year 2006, I was on a mission field for two months (June/July) while she was in her third year in her higher institution (Kogi State Polytechnic). I engaged in several exorcisms (deliverance of people who were possessed by demonic spirits) on this mission's trip. Whenever those under the oppressions of darkness were brought to me, as soon as I started praying in the name of Jesus Christ, they would fall on the ground and manifest in various forms ranging from screaming, shouting, vomiting and the likes. Peace and I were in relationship at this time. We both grew up in the same evangelical church, but she had not seen much of me ministering in this new way. I was a bit concerned because I wanted the two of us to be on the same page in our faith and beliefs. One Sunday night as I was praying, I came under the conviction of the Holy Spirit to have three days of prayer and fasting (from 6am till 6pm) for her to be endued with the power of the Holy Spirit.

Without telling her anything, I began the prayer and fasting on Monday. To my surprise, on Wednesday night, she called me on phone to narrate a story of how an elder in the same evangelical denomination came to their school Bible Study (fellowship) and gave them teaching about the need for the power of God. After his teaching, he prayed with them for God to fill them with power for effective Christian living. The whole room was filled with awesome presence of the Spirit of God. Peace came under the undeniable power of God with His giftings. Within a short time, their school Bible Study (fellowship) was filled up as people came thirsting for God. The passion for God in her was so real; she was nominated as the vice president of the fellowship Group in a short time. Even though she is a woman and from an evangelical denomination, various Pentecostal fellowships began inviting her to preach and teach in their fellowships. Everywhere she ministered, people were always coming under the conviction of sins and they repented. She became an instrument for revival throughout her campus life. By the time we got wedded in the later years, our relationship becomes like iron sharpening iron up till now. We have been doing our pastoral works for about 11 years now, in a denomination that does not allow an open display of the sign gifts. To avoid creating divisions in the church of God, we apply the wisdom of God to comply with the doctrinal beliefs and practices within our denomination and also minister among other denominations within their doctrinal beliefs and practices whenever we are invited. This makes us to be relevant, and to minister with difference both within the evangelical and Pentecostal denominations. On personal basis, God also uses our spiritual gifting to grow us in various ways. I remembered vividly, on the January 14, 2014, Peace and I went into the woods to pray. As soon as we started praising God in songs, she began to speak in tongues with interpretation at the same time. One of the personal messages the Lord gave to us was, "*get ready, I am taking you away from your church and away from this city and nation. I am preparing you for global assignment.*" We wrote down everything and God is indeed faithful to His words and promises. We are here in the States only by divine planning.

Brother Z Testimony (grafted in on permission): Sometime ago, close to fifty years now, I got to a point whereby as a preacher, I lived in guilt and self-condemnation always for preaching things that are not true in my own practical life. I said, God, I am not going to preach anymore because I'm a first-class hypocrite. I am preaching and saying things that are not true in my life. I do not want to fool people who see me stand on pulpit as a 'holy man that I am not.' I will not give up being a Christian, I love Jesus, and I know he died for me. I believe in him as the only way to the Father. But I will rather sit down at the balcony and never preach again unless you do something about me Lord. So, I went before the Lord in passionate prayer saying; I do not want gift of healing, signs and wonders. But make my inner life correspond with what I am singing and preaching. 'This is all I ask for Lord.' When I finished praying, I did not feel anything; it all looked dry, and I seemed to hit the rock bottom in my backsliding.

And then one day, when I least expected, God met me and filled me with the presence and power of the Holy Spirit suddenly. And like a postscript, he also gave me a little 'finger' called 'a gift of tongues,' on an inch long; it was not 12 feet long as it is in some churches, it a little gift of tongue. But that is not the main thing. The main thing is that something began to change in my life. And I said Lord, if this is really the fullness of the Holy Spirit, then when I read the pages of the Bible, it should look like a new book to me, because the Holy Spirit wrote it. I should see things and new revelations that I have never seen or understood in the past 16 years of my new birth that I have been studying Bible (1959-1975). I will tell you this, from the time that the Lord took me and filled me with the Holy Spirit (and I have continuously been filled with the Holy Spirit, it is not just one-time experience), I have seen some of the most amazing truths and revelations in the Scripture that I had never seen nor understood before about overcoming sin, about spiritual maturity, about building the church, and overcoming Satan and the likes.

For instance, I never knew before that time what it was to cast out demons. But since that day till now, no demon could stand before me—I cast devils out instantly from people they possessed with the authority in the name of Jesus. I never knew these things before—that Satan has been defeated and the kingdom of God is here. Jesus once said, if I cast the devils with the Spirit of God, then the kingdom of God has come (Matt 12: 28). And it really came. This truth became real in my life. This scripture does not become what I only memorized again; it became real in my life. I became encouraged and the Bible became a new book completely to me as I read and found so many revelations. It was not that I suddenly arrived at the top of a mountain in one day, but a new foundation had been laid and I began to grow upward. Again, I must be honest with you that it was not a perfect straight line; there were some little deeps, but the deeps were like on a graph that was moving upward.

I say this to encourage you. As time goes on, the deeps became less frequent and the line is getting straighten up better and better. I'm not telling you a fairy tale; it is a wonderful life.

And the most important thing the Lord showed me was, 'I allowed you to go down to the depth of defeat to teach you that I do not give the fullness of the Holy Spirit to those who think they deserve it, but to the most undeserving ones who are lowly in spirit. This cured me of ever thinking that the fullness of the Spirit is what you work for and get. There are people in some other religions who think that they have to roll on the ground to receive forgiveness of sins. Some think they must themselves in a particular river for certain number of times to be forgiven. There are others who lit up candles and pray to Mary and other gods to get forgiveness of sins. There are people who pay thousands of dollars to their religious leaders to buy forgiveness of sins. People do all kind of stuff in attempts to please their 'gods' and get something from the gods. But in this kingdom of Christ, you get it all for free—it is not based on merit. You do not get forgiveness of sin by merit, and you do not get the fullness of the Holy Spirit by merit. If God gave me the fullness of the Holy Spirit immediately when I was born again, I could have thought that I got it because I was holy and so deserve it. But God filled me when I was down and defeated to show me that the fullness of the Spirit does not come to those who deserve it but to those who need the Spirit desperately. All you need to do is to be honest about your defeated life and then yield yourself to him completely with the belief in his promise that he is ready to fill you. If you do not have faith and believe his word, you cannot get to the point of this fullness.

Revival in a whole community: Bishop Ponle Alabi (Ogbomoso, Oyo State Nigeria) and I attended the same Seminary together for our first degree in Theology, Missions and Evangelism respectively. Below is a testimony he shared with me on his Facebook page recently: *After about two hours of recording our radio program for OSBC, I wasn't too happy because two of our recorded messages were mistakenly deleted by a computer glitch. So, to take my mind off it, I got talking with my interpreter who is a missionary (we do have a couple of minutes' chat on ministry work after any recording session). The man of God told me how unresponsive the people are to the Gospel and since he is new in the area, he was trusting God for a breakthrough.*

I shared on one of the truths we shared at our discipleship meeting last year titled "Understanding how God raises worthy workers in his Harvest!" Well, he left encouraged by the truth that the Lord invites us into a harvest and it was all about His word and the Holy Spirit. He said he began to look forward to a harvest instead of labor. Just a week after his usual weekly schedules of the teaching of God's word, he returned home from his mission's field and he kept trusting that the Lord of Harvest was at work. He returned the following week and found the worship center in the remote village parked full. He was surprised because since he arrived, it was always difficult getting people to come to Church. He asked what and why the place was filled up and to his surprise, here is what he was told. After his message, a member returned home and as he prayed, the power of the Holy Spirit fell upon him and he started speaking in 'unknown tongues.' The whole villagers did not know what was going on and so they called for someone who attends Church to come help pray for the man. He arrived and as he got close to the man praying in unknown tongues, he also began to pray in strange tongues and soon the whole village gathered round to watch.

Not knowing what to do, everyone listened on and then the first man started prophesying and then speaking words of knowledge. He revealed so much that some people who were in the occult or living in sins fell down crying in repentance. You cannot but remember 1 Corinthians 14:24-25; "But if all prophesy and an unbeliever or an ungifted man enters, he is convicted by all, he is called to account by all; the secrets of his heart are disclosed; and so he will fall on his face and worship God, declaring that God is certainly among you". Praise God! The man, who was in the occult, went home and brought all his charms to be burnt and renounced his life of sins. The missionary was not even there! The village concluded that the reason for such occurrence must be the preaching of the new missionary, so everyone came to church the following Sunday. Praise God!

I do remember when something like this happened in one of our meetings last year where I shared that it was only God's word that must work. I have nothing special to share and that for them to know it was all about His word; someone will get home and be filled by God's Spirit. So, the brother got home and as he knelt down to pray, God's power fell upon him and he came back the following day shouting repeatedly-JESUS IS REAL....JESUS IS REAL. Now we know that nobody needs to depend upon us, they saw and heard the word proclaimed, and the word came alive. Our joy is in seeing the ministry of the word of grace at work.

147

An Evangelical Elder and His security man: In the year 2012, I was in Jos, Plateau State, Nigeria, for an induction course with other fellow young pastors, at the ECWA Headquarters. The clergyman that took us through the power of prayer and spiritual discipline narrated an incident that happened to a devoted elder in an evangelical church, a top government official who has a personal official driver attached to him. The security man was an unbeliever. This elder did not believe in the sign gifts of the Holy Spirit though he loves prayer so much. One day, in the middle of the night, he woke up to pray. About 25 minutes into his prayer, he started speaking in tongues unknowingly. His security man who lived in the same building woke up only to hear his boss praying in his (the security) own local dialect; but the elder (who never understood his security local language) was actually speaking in tongues. At the same moment, the security man came under the conviction of his sins and his need to accept Jesus Christ.

Early in the morning this man told his boss (the elder) that when the boss was praying yesterday, the boss was preaching to him in his (the security) local language. He told the elder that he was ready to receive that Jesus into his life. It remains mystery to the elder, but he made use of that opportunity to lead him to Christ. The

Holy Spirit cannot be caged. He works in mystery. There are thousands upon thousands of different ways in which the Spirit empowers people who are thirsty for him. The list cannot be exhausted in this book.

Do not Condemn Others' Calling, Giftings and Ministry

Just as nobody can condemn anyone for not speaking in tongues, no one is equally authorized to condemn anyone for speaking in tongues. Apostle Paul writes all do not speak in tongues, all do not have the gift of healings, all do not prophesy, all do not work miracles . . . (1 Cor. 12:27-30). The same Paul warns by saying, ". . . do not forbid speaking in tongues (1 Cor. 14:39). The Spirit who knows the strength and the need of everyone gives His gifts to all as He pleases. It is very important for you to stay in your calling and in your conviction without condemning others. Reinhard Bonnke was a Charismatic evangelist whom God has used in many nations of the world, but majorly in Africa, to reach millions of souls. In 2003, I was present in one of his crusades in Nigeria—precisely in Ilorin, Kwara State. After a powerful message of salvation, with thousands responding to the call for salvation, he prayed for the sick. In about four chairs away from me, I heard a shout of a blind man, "I can see!" In about less than one-third of a mile, I heard another shout of a crippled man "I can walk!" sooner than you could know, everywhere was filled with the awesome presence of God and with visible miracles. Bonnke was to spend five days in this city, but when the Muslims fanatics discovered that many of their women and youths were coming to the new light in Christ Jesus, they threatened to interrupt the Crusade meeting if Bonnke should continue. The incumbent governor sent an order to the Christian Association of Nigeria (CAN), Kwara Chapter to end the meeting instantly. After spending two days, Bonnke with his team left peacefully. Nevertheless, God had saved as many as He wanted these two days.

Billy Graham was an evangelical evangelist whom God used probably more than any of his contemporaries to reach millions of souls in America and across the nations of the world. He was never seen speaking in tongues nor performing miracles or healings. Yet, he was filled with the power of the Holy Spirit. Graham is not superior to Bonnke, just as Bonnke is not inferior to Graham. Both of them stayed in their callings. Poonen once said, "John Wesley and George Whitefield were two great preachers in England in the 18th century. John Wesley and his followers believed and preached that one could be lost after being saved. George Whitefield and his followers preached that once a man was saved, he was saved forever. But Wesley and Whitefield were good friends and when Whitefield died, it was Wesley who conducted his funeral. One of Wesley's followers later asked him, "Will you see George Whitefield in heaven?" John Wesley replied, "George Whitefield was so bright a star in the firmament of God's glory, and will stand so near the throne, that one like me, who am less than the least, will never catch a glimpse of him." Although Wesley's followers were narrow-hearted, Wesley himself was a humble, large-hearted man who esteemed Whitefield above himself.

In *Luke 9:49, 50*, Jesus teaches us what to do when we find someone having a ministry that is totally different from ours. Someone was casting out demons, but he did not join the disciples. John asked Jesus to stop him. But Jesus told John to leave him alone and to let him continue that ministry. You stick to your calling and let them fulfill theirs. Many Christians are so taken up with the importance of their own ministry that they feel that everyone should be doing that. *"But if the whole body were an eye, where would the hearing be; and if the whole were hearing, where would the sense of smell be?"* (*1 Corinthians 12:17*). A matured Christian realizes that God gives different ministries to different people. If one wants to do evangelism and another wants to do social work, let each fulfill his own ministry. Something of Christ can be manifested through both. But let us not destructively criticize one another. There are varieties in creation. God did not make every flower the same color, the same shape or the same size. The rainbow has so many different colors, so is the body of Christ. Narrow-minded Christians, however, never see anything other than their own ministry. Here is a word for such people: *"Thank God for every ministry and stick to your own."*

We Need One Another

The purpose of the spiritual gifts and spiritual power is for building the local church and the universal body of Christ. The Scripture does not teach that everybody in a local church must have the gift of healing and be able to heal all diseases and sickness. But within the local church or a denominational body (or another church denomination), there may be those who are gifted in administration, some in discerning of spirits, some with the gift of faith for possibilities, some are able to speak in tongues, some are blessed with the gift of divine knowledge, some with working of miracles and some with the gift of healings. In a larger scope as well, some church denomination may not emphasize the signs and healing gifts,

152

but in the Spirit of Christ, there is nothing wrong to invite a brother from another denomination who have the same beliefs in Christ and the authority of the Scripture like you, to come and teach on areas you need help and better understanding. We need one another. That a church or denomination believes in healing does not turn the denomination to an enemy of mine which does not. All the spiritual gifts are still available all over the universal body of Christ globally. The last prayer of Jesus after his resurrection was that the church all over the world will be united as one body. There may be diversities in this body, but we can have a perfect unity with all our diversities. This is to be the ultimate goal of the universal church of Christ on earth. Ego and pride have set some people on the platform of traditionalism and legalism. One of the beauties of Christianity is that there should be unity in our diversities.

Chapter10

Setting the Captives Free from their Afflictions

"That which was from the beginning, which we
have heard, which we have seen with our eyes,
which we have looked at and our hands have
touched--this we proclaim concerning the Word of
life" (1 John 1:1)

In their book, *Power Evangelism*, Wimber and Springer provide five basic factors that influence the way an average person from the Western world reacts to supernatural occurrences: rationalism, individualism, materialism, relativism and secularism. Rationalism seeks a rational explanation for all experience and explains away power evangelism. Individualism prioritizes independence and self-reliance, emphasizing one's desire to control everything. Materialism emphasizes that nothing exists except matter—that is, only what can be seen, tested and proved to be real. Hence, materialism closes the door on the supernatural and assumes that the material world is the sole reality. Relativism denies absolute truth, subjecting all truth to personal experience. Finally, secularism maintains that people live in a material world that is closed off from divine intervention.[1] The resultant effect of this fivefold Western

---

[1] John Wimber and Kevin Springer, *Power Evangelism* (Bloomington, MN: Chosen Books, 2009), 6-7.

worldview is very significant as it is tagged the "post-modern era."
Again, "because power evangelism presupposes that God still
intervenes in the affairs of men and women, the secularist rejects it
a priori."[2]

The realm of supernatural manifestation in evangelism is not
strange to African Christianity. For example, most African
worldviews seem to align better with a biblical point of view when
it comes to the realm of the spirit-world and the supernatural.[3] The
New Testament, for instance, opens with the reality of spiritual
warfare (see Matt 11:12; Luke 9:1; 10:18; John 10:10); but, at the
same time, it reveals the supremacy of the power in the gospel—
over the principalities of darkness—through the Holy Spirit. The
strong caution remains: Christians may succeed in winning people
into signs and wonders without winning them into genuine salvation
in Christ.

Here I stand

I'm neither a Pentecostal nor a charismatic believer. I'm an
evangelical who believes that when you are under the fullness of the

---

[2] Wimber and Springer, *Power Evangelism*, 7.
[3] Read more in Richard J. Gehman, *African Traditional Religion: In
the light of the Bible* (Kaduna: Baraka Press, 2000), 20-34; John S. Mbiti.
African Religions and Philosophy (New York: Fredrick A. Praeger, 1969), 1-8;
and Byang Kato, *Theological pitfalls in Africa*(Nairobi: Evangel Pub. House,
1975), 18-19.

Holy Spirit (the baptism of power), any gift or various gifts of the Holy Spirit can manifest through you as the Spirit deems fit! I believe in praying for the sick through the gift of faith (Mark 11:22-26; 1 Cor 12: 9), the gift of healing (1 Cor 12: 9) or just by simple obedience to the Scripture (James 5: 13-17)! I do not oblige to the teaching that everybody must be healed. We see cases in the scriptures of believers or people of God that remained unhealed. For instance, prophet Elisha died of sickness (2 Kings 13: 14f). Paul was not healed from his thorn after he prayed several times. Timothy was not healed from his stomach upset. Trophimus was not healed when Paul prayed for him. *"Erastus remained at Corinth: but Trophimus I left at Miletus sick"* (2 Timothy 4:20). But at the same time, I really do not know how those who claim that the age of the supernatural is gone with the apostles read their Bible to arrive at this conclusion. It is very easy to come to this conclusion though if only we do our theology within the four-walls of an office and within the four-walls of a classroom. Unlike many professors of theology today, the early apostles were always on the fields witnessing to the lost souls. Paul theology was not a theoretical one, but a product of his missional activities. Anytime we take the gospel out there where the sinners are, we will witness the power of God at work as powers and principalities of darkness bow for Jesus Christ through the workings of the Holy Spirit.

However, if God is not '**the great I was**' but '**the great I am**,' then no one can limit the miraculous workings of the Holy Spirit. He is still at work today. Someone like me can never deny the supernatural manifestation of God's power in our today's world.

There is Power in the Name of Jesus

I am glad to announce to you that **Satan our arch enemy has been disarmed, defeated, dethroned** (Col 2: 14-15) **and will at last be destroyed when he will be banished to hell** (Rev 20:10). I am like the apostles "who could never stopped proclaiming that word of life which was from the beginning, which they have heard, which they have seen with their eyes, which they have looked at and their hands have touched" (1 John 1:1 emphases is mine). Since the time I caught a glimpse of this power baptism, I was set free from the fear of the devil.

Few years back in Africa, I met a young guy who was initiated into an occult group in his high school campus. The occult name is 'Red Danger,' and he was given a name 'Satana.' The identifying slogan for this evil group is '*natas si dog*' meaning *satan is god,* if you read it in the reversed way. I took him out to an open field far away from the church to pray with him together with one of my prayer partners. At the mention of the name of Jesus, the demons in him threw him on the ground as he roared in the voice of a lion. But because of the finished work of Christ on the Cross, he was delivered and set free.

Peace (my wife) counseled a young girl one time that belonged to a demonic group in school. The name of this group is 'MUD' (Meet them, Use them, Drop them). This group consists of young girls who had reached the age of adolescence. This girl was the recruiting officer for the group. A lot of young girls were initiated into this group and they engaged in wild sexual activities. Their primary aim was to seduce young boys and men and lure them into sexual promiscuities with the target to destroy their destiny demonically. After Peace led her to Christ, we prayed with her with the authority in the Name of Jesus. With all her perverse sexual stories, God delivered her completely and she is fine till date—married with children.

A young Christian girl was enticed by a Muslim guy with voodoo power. She ran away from home for months without the knowledge of her whereabouts. The parents called me requesting for prayers. We began an intercessory prayer on her behalf. Few days after we began the prayer, she was located at the hideout where she was cohabiting with her sexual partner. She was brought home, but her soul had been caged and needed to be detached. We brought her to our church prayer room to cast out the demon out of her in the name of Jesus. When we began praying, I saw the Spirit of God printing an Islamic name 'Hadijah' in my mind. I tried to annul this to concentrate on the prayer, but the name kept coming again and again. Then I paused the prayer and asked her of her connection to this name. She told us that she had been initiated to Islamic religion with all rituals and rites performed upon her. During the initiation, her Christian name was changed and the name 'Hadijah' was given to her. I commanded authoritatively the satanic spirit behind this name to lose its power and let her go. At this junction, she shouted violently like a wild donkey. The Spirit of the Lord broke the chain that held her captive and she was set free. There is power in the name of Jesus.

I met another guy whose story was enough to make a whole book. He was initiated into a secret cult "Aye fraternity." He was given the name 'Idris Aloma,' and he was the PRO for the fraternity. Just at the moment we were praying for this young man after he accepted Jesus Christ into his life, his phone rang. Guess who was calling him? It was the leader of the group whose name was 'Aye Desmond Tutu.' His voice sound threatening, as he commanded our new convert to call an emergency meeting for the following day. Our new convert was fidgeting and was schizophrenically afraid. Then I said, "tell him that you are not going to call any meeting; and that you have found a new Master whose name is Jesus Christ; and that he too needs the same Jesus Christ". But he was afraid to say that, because he assured us that they would come after him to kill him. Anyway, I encouraged him to say that. Then the guy at the other end of the phone said in a thunderous voice; "you will pay for this." Then, he hung off the phone. The rest of the story was pathetic for this group leader (Aye Desmond Tutu), because he died in the following week when his group clashed with another group in a serious occultic battle. As we were praying for this guy (named Idris Aloma), I heard in my spirit, "there is charm (voodoo power) on him." He answered yes; and asked how did you know? Down beneath his underwear was hidden a 'magical cowry' with some black item attached. With this on him, gunshot, dagger, cutlass and other deadly weapons will not be able to harm him. As I commanded in the name of Jesus, the power of the Lord lifted him up in the air and he went flat on the floor. He manifested and got delivered by Jesus Christ.

I preached at the wedding program of a chorister. Few months after her wedding, she thought she was pregnant because of all the signs of morning sickness she was experiencing. But each time she went to the gynecologists for test and examinations, they kept telling her there was not any pregnancy in her. She got to a point where she was confused and came over for prayer. A drama happened at the gate of our church with our security men. I was in my apartment with my wife, but the two church security men (for the daytime) told her that I drove out of the church premises a moment ago. They wanted to turn her back, but she refused. After much argument with them, she decided to call my cell phone. To the surprise of the security men, I was at home. Anyway, she came, and we decided to pray in our sitting room.

In the cause of our interaction with her before prayer, we made her renounce her covenant with the dark world and confess her allegiance to Christ Jesus. Then, as we commanded her to be free in Jesus name, a manly voice spoke through her saying, "she is my queen, she belongs to me, and no one can take her away from me." Then, in a violent manifestation, she removed her wedding ring and threw it away. We announced to that force of darkness that that was then; she now belongs to Jesus the bridegroom who had paid her bride price with his blood. The demon left instantly and till today, she is free and serving the living God. The devil doesn't like to be reminded of his defeat on the cross. That same day, she went back to the hospital where she was told that she was three months pregnant already.

I was invited to preach one time at a certain youths' meeting. There was a particular boy who was among those who made decision for salvation, requested to see me privately. He narrated how he was overpowered by the spirit of immorality so much that he was into bestiality. He wondered if Jesus could forgive all his awful past and ugly life and set him free. Of course, Jesus did; and he is free till today. "Whomever the Son of God set free is free indeed". A girl was bed-wetting for 16 years; the Lord delivered her by the authority in His Name.

On a particular campus, a certain girl was battling with asthmatic cough that always put her to shame anywhere she turned. Joining hands to pray with her with Peace, I heard a voice in me saying; 'she's guilty of blood.' I paused to ask her what was going on; then she confessed that she aborted a baby recently. Alright, we turned the direction of the prayer to asking for mercy and cleansing by the blood of Jesus. Innocent blood always cries for vengeance like the blood of Abel (Heb 12: 24; cf Deut 21:1-7; Rev 17:6). Confession and repentance are the way out of the guilt of sin (1 John 1:7-9). She came under the conviction of sin and cried like a little baby. The Lord pardoned her and healed her instantly. She is doing well today—she's married and with children. I can write a whole book on the power on the victories we have witnessed as Jesus Christ set people free from bondage. There are still several people in bondages in our churches and around us that need to be set free. Therefore, you and I need the baptism of power. We need to rise to our duties.

Forgiveness sets them Free

I have heard of sudden disappearance of goiter when a woman forgave the person she needed to forgive. I have witnessed several long-time barrenness cases terminated when couples learned how to forgive one another. Tumors of various kinds have been healed without surgical operations when the victims surrendered their lives to Christ and forgave their debtors. Victims of high blood pressure and other related body and life-threatening diseases easily received their healings and sound health back when they forgave. A woman received her joy and freedom back, with tears rushing down her cheeks, after she forgave a senior colleague in the office who debarred her of promotion over twenty-five years ago when this senior colleague hid one of the documents vital to her promotion. So, for over twenty-five years, she was carrying a pregnancy of hatred and enmity. Her experience reveals the high cost of living in unforgiveness because you will lose many things when you refuse to forgive. You lose fellowship with God, you lose your relationship with men, and your wealth and your health are at stake when you cannot forgive. Truly speaking, you cannot enjoy your wealth and health if your life is ramped up in the cage of unforgiveness. On forgiveness, you can read more in my book "Beyond Forgiveness" on Amazon.

Prayer that Works

In praying for anyone under the oppression of the devils, Peace and I have adopted the guidelines below.

- We thank God for His love, the finished work of Christ on the Cross and for his power available for us today.

- We pray with clear conscience; without hidden sins (Psalm 66:18; Mark 11:23-25; James 1:6-8)

- We pray with boldness and an unwavering faith (Mark 11:22-23)

- We pray fervently (James 5:17)

- We prayer persistently (1 Kings 18: 43; Luke 18:1f; 2 Corinthians 12:8)

- We pray with fasting or self-denial of personal pleasures (Acts 13:1-3)

- We pray in the strength and power of the Holy Spirit (Luke 4:1; Jude 20)

- We pray authoritatively in the NAME of Jesus Christ (John 14:12-14)

- We pray expectantly in the will of God (Matt 26: 42)

- We give praises and thanks to God after prayer (Matt.5:12; 6: 13; Eph 6: 19-20; Phil.4:6)

- Then, we leave the result (Yes/No/Wait) unto God

Chapter 11

The Lack in the Church Today

". . . having a form of godliness but denying its power. Have nothing to do with such people" (2 Timothy 3: 5)

The lack in the Church today is not musical instruments, electronic gadgets, money, and other material resources. In fact, in some countries, there are church denominations that are richer than a whole state. The lack in the Church today is not intellectuals. As a matter of fact, the Church is filled up with men that are experts in expository and exegetical sermons, because there are many Bible commentaries, Greek and Hebrew lexicons, and other ready-made materials on the internet. The Church does not lack talents. There are many talented but unregenerated singers and instrumentalists all over churches today. But today, the Church lacks power and spiritual authority due to *prayerlessness*. The Church is full of manpower but lacking in God's power. Pathetically to say, today, our sermons lack transforming power because they are products of head knowledge and for mental stimulations. What is the use of our expository sermons without the transforming power? We are no longer seeing converts—sinners turning away from sins and laying down their lives on the altar after our Sunday morning sermons all because most at times, our sermons are not birthed on the altar of prayer and power. Today, Satan has succeeded in weakening the spiritual life of the Church by lack of commitment to passionate prayer life that birth power. The devil knows that a prayer-less church is a powerless church. Most of the Wednesdays of the week are scheduled for Bible Study in most of the Churches in United States, but there are no special days for prayer meeting within the week. The prayer meeting time is gradually fading away from the church. I'm afraid we might hand over 'Christianity without power' due to prayerlessness to the oncoming generation.

In Jeremiah 15: 1, God calls attention to two reputable men of prayer in the Old Testament, Moses and Samuel. You quite remember that it was Moses standing in gap before the Lord that left Israel with remnants that entered the Promised Land. The Israelites rebelled against God ten times; Moses interceded for them ten times. God answered Moses prayers nine times. Prophet Samuel told the Israelites, '*As for me, far be it from me that I should sin against the LORD by failing to pray for you. And I will teach you the way that is good and right*' (1Samuel 12: 23). Throughout Samuel's days, the Israelites served the Lord. Worthy to note here is that the prayer of these two prophets of God did not center on personal needs—money, material, health or wealth, no. They wrestled with God for the preservation of Israelite souls. Someone rightly says prayer is entering with God for the souls of men; and coming out with men for God. Prayer is partnering with God to bring God's will down on earth.

Constantinople and Northern Africa were predominantly Christian worlds. But when the Church fathers and apologists substituted prayer for intellectualism and scholasticism; internal pollution and baseless arguments became the order of the day, and Christianity in those regions was almost wiped out by non-Christians. The Church today is again heading into the same situation. We need to wake up. What happens when the Church fails to pray? Godly nations begin to backslide; anti-Bible laws become the order of the day; souls perish every day when the Church fails to pray; the Church will be filled up with nominal Christians who come to church on Sunday-Sunday basis without leaving their lives of sin behind; younger generation stray from the path of righteousness; Church members become prey when there is no prayer and backslide into the mire of sin.

The backsliding rate of Christians today is so alarming (cf Matt 24: 12). Apostle Paul always prayed for the spiritual firmness of all churches (Eph 1:15-23; 3:14-21; Phil 1:7-9; Col 1:9-12). The Church becomes lukewarm, carnality sets in, the church turns to charity organizations, and the church becomes dead (spiritually), and becomes an entertainment ground. There are places today where church buildings (including members) are being offered for sale. The Church becomes a toothless dog that cannot bite, and not be able to challenge anti-Bible laws. The Christian heritage of any nation can be eroded when men stop to pray. Let it not be as someone has opined that the Church is "too far gone ever to be revived." Are you rightly positioned in God's agenda in this End Time? The failure of the Church is our failure in prayer. Someone rightly puts it, *the early Church began with men in upper room agonizing, but the Church is ending today with men in the supper room organizing.* God will hold us responsible for the spiritual decay of the Church. In his day, John Knox of Scotland wrestled in prayers. On his knees he would pray "Lord...! give me Scotland or else I die." In his days, there was much reverence for God. John Hyde's name was changed to Praying Hyde because of his several hours of prayer on his knees every day. He was an American Missionary to India; he believed that the seed of prayer never dies. He interceded to the end of his life for India position, several years later, an evangelist went there and preached for just ten minutes and about three million people surrendered their lives to Christ. I am not talking of casual 'baby' prayer—but serious intercessory hours before the Lord. The fervent and effective prayer of a righteous man is powerful (James 5:16-17). By the passionate and zealous prayer of the early church, the Apostle Peter was miraculously set free from prison, the word of God grew and prevailed all over the land (Acts 12:1-9). The lack in the church today is fervent and effective prayer; and a prayerless church is a powerless church. A prayerless church is a weak church; a prayerless church is a fruitless church.

Go for the Power in the Word

The apostle Paul says, *For I resolved to know nothing while I was with you except Jesus Christ and him crucified. I came to you in weakness with great fear and trembling. My message and my preaching were not with wise and persuasive words, but with a demonstration of the Spirit's power, so that your faith might not rest on human wisdom, but on God's power* (1 Cor. 2: 2-5). Today, as I have mentioned, that in the strive for biblical expositions of several bible scholars, we have left the transforming power out. The academic analysis and exegesis of the Bible is good. However, preachers must wait on their kneels for transformative power

170

through the Holy Spirit. Else, our academic exegesis of the Bible may erode the revelational and transformational power of the word of God away. Jesus never questioned the Old Testament. He was not bothered by what all the theologians and the critics (Pharisees and Sadducees) of His days said. He believed the Scripture, and he experienced its power. Today, the devil is leading so many people astray from such simple faith. Instead of believing God's word and thus experiencing the power therein, some go ahead to use their cleverness and smartness to analyses Scripture and waste their entire lives without experiencing the power of God. How do you want to live? *Do you want to live analyzing the Scripture or experiencing the power of God through it? The choice is yours.* Mary submitted to God's word and said, *"Let it be done to me according to your word"* (Lk 1:38).

Chapter 12

The Balance of Truth

I, even I, have spoken; yes, I have called him. I have brought him, and he will succeed in his mission. Come near to me and listen to this: From the beginning I have not spoken secret; from the time it happened, I was there. And now the Lord GOD has sent me, accompanied by His Spirit (Isa 48: 16).

The word of God and the Spirit of God always work together. We see this at the Creation. We also see this during the inauguration of Jesus ministry as earlier mentioned. Hence, when you place emphasis on the power of the Holy Spirit without placing a commensurate emphasis on the word, there will always be imbalances in your beliefs and practices. The same thing goes with placing emphasis on the word and neglecting the place of the Holy Spirit.

Value the Word of God

The word of God sets boundary for the Spirit's move. The operation of the Spirit's power without the balanced word of God is dangerous. This is why both the word and the Spirit do not operate in isolation (Isaiah 48:16). Power without the word of truth leads to heretical teachings and spiritism. For instance, one of the reasons we have so many false prophets, prophetesses, preachers and church founders (or General Overseers) in many parts of Africa today is because most of these people place undue emphasis on prayer and fasting with less attention on digging deep in the Word. My fellow Christian brothers and sisters in Nigeria, for example, are fond of going into prayer and fasting for seven days, fourteen days, twenty-one days, forty days, ninety days and one-hundred and twenty days. But less attention is given to the word of God and, no wonder; most of the prayer requests on prayer grounds and prayer mountains are so unbiblical. Most of the independent church owners pour contempt on seminary education. Some of them give their members six weeks, three-four months training and go ahead to ordain them as pastors, evangelists, prophets and leaders. The dangers that some of these half-baked workers have done to the Christianity in most parts of Africa is becoming almost irreparable. Let consider few of some of the heretical practices.

A well-known pastor sometimes ago said he was under the leading of the Holy Spirit when he brought a rod to the pulpit and commanded the audience to keep their gaze to the rod as they make their prayers to God. The truth is Jesus Christ has been lifted up on the Cross. We can no longer go to the time of Moses in the wilderness. At the beginning of a new year, an African preacher once told his members to buy hair combs to church for special prayer. Some came with bags and load of combs. After the man of God finished praying upon the combs, he told the members to use one comb each to comb their head backwards several times with a repetitive word of prayer; "I comb away all the evil in this new year." This to him is a symbol that the members have ward off and avert all evils for the year. This is part of the modern days' syncretic practices. Unfortunately, many of those who came with bags of the comb began to ship them out to foreign countries where there are Nigerians and began to sell them as the 'anointed combs' that a respectable man of God from Nigeria had blessed. This became a source of income or business for them.

I was in a commercial bus with a particular lady one time. Just when our bus was about to board, she came out of the bus and flagged down a commercial motorcyclist to take her back home to go and pick the bottle of oil which she forgot at home. Why she attached so much importance on the oil was because her General Overseer (G.O) had prayed over the oil and that the oil is another Holy Spirit in a bottle. She believed that this anointing oil would serve many purposes ranging from protection, favor, blessing to healing and the likes. I have seen some prophets who told women who are looking for fruits of the wombs to go and bring their under wears (undies) for special prayer so that they would be able to conceive. Some of these prophets will tell people to bring salt, honey, and some other items for prayer. What they do is to chant some passages in Psalms to these items and give them back to the people with prescription on how to use them. This is purely an act of idolatry. I have equally seen some prophets giving out beads or other items to people telling them to pray with or through these items like a Muslim make use of tasbih (Muslim prayer beads) or as a Catholic man will pray to 'God' using rosary bead. Praying to God through an object or through any human being on earth is not found in the New Testament. Christians are to pray to God through Jesus Christ alone. It is true we read in the book of Acts that the shadow of Peter healed the sick (Acts 5: 15-18). Handkerchiefs or aprons that touched the apostle Paul healed the sick and cast out evil spirits from the people. But such items were not idolized (Acts 19: 12).

A friend of mine was invited by a friend to his Church during his Church's special prayer meeting that was coupled with fasting. At the middle of the prayer, "the man of God" said, "It is now time for the business of the day." At this juncture, everybody began to open his or her pocket and bag to bring out either picture or a piece of cloth. Little did he know that 'the man of God' (MOG) had told the people on the first day of the prayer to come with any item or material belonging to anyone they know is their enemy, who is hindering their progress in life. The pews were filled to the brim as people queued before this man of God who brought out a bottle of oil and was anointing those materials and shouting **'Holy Ghost fire; consume them; Die! Die!! Die!!!'** By this act, he convinced them that those enemies would die between 7 to 14 days. The person my friend followed to that Church brought out the picture that carried his own father's face. He also joined in calling 'Holy Ghost fire' to consume his father since many prophets and prophetesses had convinced him that his own father was the one behind his misfortune. What a big deception! I usually call these types of prophets "modernized spiritualists, herbalists or hired religious 'assassins.'[1] You cannot find any of these practices in the New Testament church nor among any of the apostles of Christ. All of these are borrowed from some of the practices in African Traditional Religions. These few examples portray how shallow is

---

[1] See more of these in my book Beyond Forgiveness at:
https://www.amazon.com/Beyond-Forgiveness-Tunde-Abednego-Samuel-ebook/dp/B07PK5C2J4/ref=sr_1_1?dchild=1&keywords=Tunde+Samuel+Beyond+Forgiveness&qid=1605548520&s=books&sr=1-1

the scriptural knowledge these so-called men of God. This also can be a result of pseudo conversion or lack of thorough discipleship after conversion. Nevertheless, I have seen few church leaders who are doing well in ministry despite the fact that they have never gotten seminary education, but who have spent quality time in the word of God with dedication, commitment and self-discipline. The place of prayer is different from the place of the Word. You need the balance of the two or else you will become a false prophet.

When you emphasize the Word without the power

When we place emphasis on the correctness of biblical interpretation (sound doctrine) without the practical emphasis and the brooding of the Spirit to release power upon us, we can easily fall into the error of legalism and traditionalism. This is the error of the Pharisees in the days of Jesus. The Pharisees had a correct doctrine (the law of Moses) so much that Jesus admonishes people to follow what the Pharisees taught. But they have a wrong lifestyle and were empty of the power that brings transformation. Hence, they lack freshness in their teaching. The fact remains that the letters of the law kill (2 Cor. 3:6) when the presence of the Holy Spirit is not there. Most of the time in the evangelical circles, our main emphasis centers on expository and exegetical sermons, but we always forget to talk about the expository power. In United States for instance, there are several cathedrals all over the place. But when you get inside on Sundays, the populations are so scanty. Some friends of mine have been in churches with big structures but found less than 30 worshipers there who are mostly aged people.

The mass movement of the youths away from American churches for example, is highly alarming, and this is evident in many surveys carried out in recent times.[2] Several attempts are in the pipeline to curb this drift. Some Seminaries introduced Church Revitalization as a course into the theological curriculums. Some organizations are ready to finance and support church planters. In addition, several churches have various sport facilities within the church premises as strategy to attract the youths to the church. These and other methodologies sound great and deserve kudos. The truth however remains that the basic factor about the youths' exodus has not been addressed. Until the churches give prominent attention to the practical ministry of the Holy Spirit in the church, the problem remains unsolved. There is nothing in this wide world that can satisfy the pant and thirst in the souls of the hungry youths of this

---

[2] Pew Research findings talk a lot on this.

generation except the outpouring of the Holy Spirit's power upon them (Joel 2:28; Acts 2:18).

Someone once wrote a book with the caption; *Where is the Church when the Youths went astray?* This same question is still very relevant today. We need to start teaching about the power of the Holy Spirit that can break and replace the inordinate addictions of our youths to cell phones, internet, sexual perversions, sports, drugs and other vices at the detriment of their own spiritual life. This traditionalism in our churches today that is void of spiritual power will not help us. It is time to go and add to our expository preaching the practical expository power in the gospel, and the power that comes through the touch of the Holy Spirit. Remember Paul's words again, "my message and my preaching were not in persuasive words of wisdom [using clever rhetoric, not a display of eloquence], but [they were delivered] in demonstration of the Holy Spirit [operating through me] and of [His] power [stirring the minds of the listeners and persuading them], so that your faith would not rest on the wisdom *and* rhetoric of men, but on the power of God" (1 Cor 2: 4-5 Amp emphasis is mine).

Chapter 13

How to Receive this Power

Ask and it will be given to you; seek and you will
find; knock and the door will be opened to you
(Matt 7:7)

As I have mentioned, sometimes, this baptism of power comes along with a genuine conversion. Right from the point of their conversion, some are endowed with power, and if you ever meet anyone with this power, you will know he or she possesses it. Similarly, if this power is at work in your life, you do not need to make a noise before it becomes glaring; and you will know that you have it. If you once had it and lost it along the way, go back on your kneels in humility and ask God for it. Stop telling the story of past or lost glory. I will itemize few things below as steps to receiving this baptism. Some of the things I will be mentioning are interwoven with some of the points I have discussed in the earlier chapters of this book.

Believe it is available for you

If you are a cessationist who claim that some of the gifts— especially the sign gifts of the Holy Spirit have ceased; then to log into the fullness of this power will be very difficult because of skepticism and sometimes, you will always find emptiness within you. You will always be full of doubt and agitation and may always tag those who are gifted in these areas as heretics. The fact that we have a lot of fakes does not deny the existence of the original. Every one of us has a particular assignment at a particular location where God has called us into. The need of a missionary working in the interior part of the Arab world may differ from that of a preacher in a big city in Texas. Whatever your assignment is and wherever your place of duty is; you need the power of the Holy Spirit to carry out your mandate to the fullest. When Mary asked the angel about how she would be able to do the herculean task the angel spoke about, angel Gabriel answered by saying; "the Holy Spirit will come on you, and the power of the Most High will overshadow you" (Luke 1:35).

It is true for instance that the Bible says that tongues will cease, that is, they will come to a stop at one time (1 Cor 13). The time when tongues cease to function is not however indicated anywhere in the Bible. Some scholars came up with various positions on this though. Byang Kato once observes, "however, this is one area where I cannot be dogmatic in as many eminent Bible scholars do not all agree on this. I can only say that tongues will certainly cease. Since the time is not indicated, it is possible that they have ceased. But it is also possible that genuine tongues are still in use and will one-day cease."

The prophecy of Joel quoted in Acts 2:17-21 can be used to support the possibility of tongues still in use. The last days in Scriptures may refer to the whole period of grace from the time of Christ's first coming till the end of this age at His second coming. The widespread charismatic movement today may have both the genuine and the counterfeit experiences. But the Word of God, and not the experience itself, should be the standard for judgment.'[1] I personally opine that as long as the Holy Spirit still dwells in the midst of the church of Christ, his gifts (the Spirit's gifts) will continue to manifest through the believers in Christ as the Holy Spirit chooses. However, gift or no gift, everybody needs power to fulfill the spiritual assignment allotted to him or her in this world of satanic and demonic powers. Can you agree with me by saying; "Lord, I believe, I need your power." Let this conviction sink down in your heart. As you believe this truth, you also receive the baptism by faith.

---

[1] See Byang Kato, "The Power of the Holy Spirit," in *Today's Challenge* (Jos: Challenge Publication, September/October 1974), 4f

Pray for this baptism of Power

One of the reasons I title this book 'the Baptism of Power of the Holy Spirit' is because, the Scripture does not teach Christians to be praying for Holy Spirit. The Holy Spirit comes to dwell in you at the point of your new birth (regeneration). The Apostle Paul says, *'no one who is speaking by the Spirit of God says, "Jesus be cursed," and no one can say, "Jesus is Lord except by the Holy Spirit"* (1 Cor 12:3). The only reason why you call Jesus your Lord is because the Holy Spirit dwells in you. Good Muslims call Jesus all sort of good names as they see it in their Qur'an. But they find it difficult to call Jesus Lord just because they do not have the Holy Spirit residing in them.

Beginning from Jesus, after his baptism, Jesus was said to be praying. Praying for what? Praying to be anointed by the Spirit. This we know for sure because his prayers were always answered immediately—and we see here the answer to his prayer as the Holy Spirit descended upon him. No wonder Jesus said, . . . *how much more will your Father in heaven give the Holy Spirit to those who ask him!"* (Lk 11:13). Hence, we can see clearly at this point that Jesus himself received the anointing of the Holy Spirit as an answer to prayer. This is the same for us all. If we acknowledge that we lack God's power (Acts 1:8) and that the rivers of living water are not flowing out through us (John 7:38) and seek God in prayer (Lk 11:13)—then we too will be able to accomplish a mighty ministry for God on earth through the fullness of the Spirit.

Let us examine Luke 11:13 in its context. If you are a child of God, I want you to know that God is more than eager to fill you with the Holy Spirit than you are eager to be filled with the Holy Spirit. In Luke 11:11-13, Jesus said, *"If a son asks for bread from any father among you, will he give him a stone? Or if he asks for a fish, will he give him a serpent instead of a fish? Or if he asks for an egg, will he offer him a scorpion? If you then, **being evil**, know how to give good gifts to your children, how much more will your heavenly Father give the Holy Spirit to those who ask Him!"* *(NKJV)*

As a matter of fact, before my children ask for breakfast, I get them ready, calling them one by one to come and pick their food. They do not need to ask most times. The phrase *"**you being evil...**"* means that the best father on earth is evil compared to the goodness of the Lord. In other words, the level of your love for your child is way below the level of the love of God for His children.

Yet, 'an evil earthly father (for instance) knows how to give good gift to his child, how much more will God—the Heavenly

Father gives the Holy Spirit (that's the fullness or the power of the Holy Spirit) to those who ask Him. But the issue is, unlike a good earthly father who give food to his child even before the child asks, why does the Lord wait for us to ask before He gives us what we need (cf Matt 7:7; Luke 11:9-10)? Why does your heavenly Father who always knows what you need (Matt 6:), yet he wants you to ask.? God says you need to ask for the power of the Holy Spirit before you receive. God doesn't give His gift to those who do not know the value or those who will not value it. Jesus once said, *"Do not give dogs what is sacred; do not throw your pearls to pigs. If you do, they may trample them under their feet, and turn and tear you to pieces" (Matt 7:6).*

Consider the forgiveness of sin for instance, which is the first step to being filled with the Holy Spirit. Forgiveness of sin is very essential for every human being. God does not want any man to perish (2 Peter 3: 9). God wants all human beings to be saved (1 Timothy 2:4). But why doesn't God forgive all their sins? No! Why? Because God does not force anything on people or what they do not want. He expects everyone to come to Him to ask for forgiveness. God wants you to value his gift for you. When our hands are full of other things, we do not have any hand left to receive what God has for us. You try to give a dollar to a child or baby whose hands have grasped cookies, you will see that the child will not be able to receive the dollar because the child is not ready to straighten the hands to let go of the cookies in his or her hands. Similarly, there are many things that we have held tightly unto that we may need to let go out of our hands or hearts to be able to receive the fullness of the Holy Spirit. Sometimes, we have to let go of our selfishness, reputation, pride in our dead works, ego, unforgiveness, worldly smartness etc. and become empty so that the Spirit can fill us to the brim. How much of you do you yield to the Holy Spirit?

Again, the message of Christ as we see in Luke 11 is talking about asking for the fullness of the Holy Spirit. How should we ask? This is not just a casual asking; it is a fervent asking. Jesus used two illustrations to drive his point home on this. First, the illustration of a father giving something to a child who asked. This demonstrates the love of our Heavenly Father who is ever ready to pour out His Spirit upon us when we ask. The second illustration demonstrates how fervently we should ask. In Luke 11: 5f shows a man whose friend came late in the mid night. This man went to his neighbor to ask for food for his hungry friend. ". . . *A friend of mine has just arrived for a visit, and I have nothing for him to eat.' And suppose he calls out from his bedroom, 'Don't bother me. The door is locked for the night, and my family and I are all in bed. I can't help you.' But I tell you this—though he won't do it for friendship's sake, if you keep knocking long enough, he will get up and give you whatever you need because of your shameless persistence* (Luke 11: 6-8NLT). Even though this neighbor said, 'do not bother me . . .,' because this man loves his friend so much, he would not go but kept knocking persistently (verse 8).

Hence, a thorough exegesis of Luke 11:13 and when compared with other scriptures reveal that a believer in Christ Jesus does not need to keep asking for the Holy Spirit after conversion. But a believer can ask to be filled with the Holy Spirit at any point in time. The receiving of the Holy Spirit comes at the point of regeneration (see1 Cor 12:3; II Cor 5:17), but the filling of the Holy Spirit wherein lies the power is a continuous occurrence.[2] In this parable of Luke 11, Jesus taught his disciples to talk to God as their Father. This was revolutionary, because no-one in Israel's history had ever addressed God as 'Dad' (which is the real meaning of the Hebrew word 'Abba'). In addition to addressing God as Jehovah,

---

[2] Zac Poonen, *Through the Bible: A Message for Today from every Book of the Bible*, 599.

today we are to relate with Him as Father. You want to pause and pray now to your heavenly father for this power!

Again, the man (in the parable above) was not even asking for himself, but for the need of another person. The same thing the fullness of the Holy Spirit does in our lives apart from victorious living is to become a blessing that flow to others' lives like river of living waters that refreshes you and flow to others. This man was not asking for himself and his family. If you do not have concerns for other people, then forget about the fullness of the Holy Spirit. But if you want to be a river of living waters that flows to others whom you are called to serve in the body of Christ (John 7:37-39), then you need to ask until you are filled. Hence, we should never stop asking until we are endued with this power (Luke 11:9-10). Jesus gave us a similar story of persistency in prayer in Luke 18: 1-8.

Personal Story

During my last year in my first theological Seminary (ECWA Theological Seminary Iguana, Nigeria), I began seeking the face of the Lord persistently in prayers and fasting, asking him for the fullness of his power. I felt within me that though my head had been loaded with various theological views during my four years' rigorous studies in the Seminary; I still felt an emptiness in me that needed to be filled. Most of the time during my fasting days, I will go inside the chapel, lay on the carpet bedside the pulpit and pray for hours. At a particular week (during the Seminary spiritual week of emphasis), I had three consecutive dreams in a row. In my first dream, I saw an elegantly looking old man with a bottle of oil passing in front of me. Then, I shouted as I beckoned on him saying; 'old man, this is the oil I have been longing for'. He stopped and motioned to me saying; 'bring your vessel (container) to get from the oil'.

Unfortunately, the only container I could lay hand on around me was a basket (an African type of basket with holes all around). The man said, 'son, if I pour the oil in this container, it will leak and this oil is so precious that a drop of it must not be wasted.' Then I said, 'please old man do not go yet. Let me look for another container.' He waited. I searched round but could not find any container. I saw a small tree with large leaves and I plucked some of the leaves. I then put these leaves as lining inside the basket and rushed back to the old man saying, 'I have put some lining now, please pour the oil'. He looked at me and said, 'son, even if I pour the oil, your container will still leak'. Then I woke up from the dream sweating. I cried to God for victory over my besetting sins and began to ask for cleansing.[3] As you keep asking, keep checking your life to sanitize it and keep it pure for the Spirit (Rom 12: 1-2).

Make purity your pursuit

In John 14: 30, Jesus said, ". . . for the ruler of this world is coming, and he has nothing in Me." Satan could lay no claim on any sin with which to accuse Jesus of. Sins create a legal ground for satanic afflictions. In purity lies your security. In *Hebrews 5:7*, we are told of how Jesus prayed *"in the days of His flesh. "He "prayed with loud crying and tears to be saved from death. "* This is not referring to the last day of His life when He prayed in Gethsemane only. God's Word makes it clear that Jesus prayed like that *"in the days of His flesh. "* Here, *"Days"* refers to His entire 33½ years on earth. The death that Jesus prayed to be saved from (and from which He was saved, as this verse says) was certainly not physical death, but spiritual death, which results from committing even one sin. Jesus prayed that He might never sin even once; he prayed that he might stay in the will of God all his life. He was so earnest about

---

[3] Please do not go and use this personal testimony of mine to go and build theology about anointing oil. I believe and rely on the filling of the Holy Spirit rather than going to buy physical bottle of oil and begin to pour it on people. For personal reason and conviction, I am not used to olive (anointing oil), I only pray with people in the 'Name of Jesus.' God used this dream or revelation to point out the carnality in my life, and I repented.

this, that His prayers for help were with loud crying and tears. That is why He never sinned.

Many imagined that Jesus overcame sin because He was the Son of God. No. He overcame sin because He prayed with loud crying and tears to be saved from sin because he lived 100% as man with flesh and blood like you and me. Therefore, the Scriptures affirms it that "he had to be made like his brothers and sisters, fully human in every way . . . (Hebrews 2:17). Jesus came in the flesh, and he was tempted like us in every way (Hebrews 4: 15; 1 John 4:1-3). But He loved righteousness and hated sin so earnestly that He prayed so fervently – and His Father **anointed Him with power** (*Hebrews 1:9*). *"Jesus hated sin, because it would break His fellowship with His Father."*

Most believers take sin casually and assume that they can never overcome sin, because they are human. But that is not the reason. The reason is that *they do not pray with loud crying and tears to be saved from sin.* It was to pray with loud crying and tears that Jesus often sought out lonely places for prayer (*Luke 5:16*). When we live in the city, it is difficult to find a lonely place. But I have discovered that I can pray with loud crying in my heart to God, without making any sound with my mouth, wherever I may be. I can

191

cry out for purity in thoughts, words, and deeds. And if I fall into some sin, I want to have tears. Jesus never fell and yet He had tears. That really humbles me. Zeal for purity consumed Jesus and burned Him up. That is why He accomplished all the will of God on earth. The fullness of the Holy Spirit brings a zeal for purity within us. Then we can follow Jesus' example. Jesus faced the same temptations that we all face every day (Heb.4:15). He had all our limitations, and yet he overcame—because he loved righteousness and hated sin and cried out to the Father for help whenever he was tempted (Heb.1:9; 5:7). The Holy Spirit helped Jesus as a Man - and the Holy Spirit will help you also in the same way.

But the good news is, you do not need to be perfect or totally overcome all sins in your life before God anoints you with the power. As a matter of fact, you need the baptism of power to be able to overcome sins. We do not try to put the cart before the horse. However, there must be a desire in your heart to hate sins with all passion before the baptism follow.

Unforgiveness and bitterness

I have talked about the need to keep yourself pure to receive this baptism of power (the fullness of the Spirit). But let me hint more on bitterness and unforgiveness. According to Luke, the Holy

Spirit descended on Jesus Christ in bodily form like a dove (Luke 3:21-22). A dove is a bird without a gallbladder. A gallbladder contains a bitter acidic content. My take in this is that you cannot have the Holy Spirit residing in you and be dominated with bitterness, hatred and unforgiveness toward your fellow brother or sister. Romans 5:5 says, 'the love of Christ is spread abroad in our heart,' hence, there should not be any room for hatred. All the gifts of the Spirit work genuinely in the body of Christ only through love (Gal 6:2). This is why the Apostle Paul devoted a whole chapter of 1 Corinthians 13 teaching on love, in between two chapters of his teachings on the spiritual gifts (1 Cor 12 and 14). Always remember, "but if you do not forgive men their sins, neither will your Father forgive your sins (Matt 6:15).

Value Fellowship with the Father like Jesus did

Jesus was never afraid of physical death. But he feared spiritual death, and so he never wanted even the smell of sin in him at any time. What was he praying for in Gethsemane when he said; *"My Father, if it is possible, may this cup be taken from me. Yet not as I will, but as you will'* (Matt 26:39). The cup he feared was the **break of fellowship with His Father for six hours** on the cross – when he would bear our sin. That is spiritual death. Right from eternity past, Jesus Christ had never broken fellowship with the Father. But in Gethsemane, the Father told Him that he would have to accept that break in fellowship, if he was to save others from eternal separation from God in hell. And in His immense love for us, Jesus agreed to pay that heavy price. But all through his life He had resisted any break of fellowship with the Father – that would come through sin. If we value that fellowship, we will also pray with loud cry and tears that there should not be in us, the slightest smell of bitterness, spiritual pride, impurity, jealousy, love of money, hatred, or anything outside the perfect will of God.

When you are immersed in the Holy Spirit, you will get to a point where you value the fellowship with the Holy Spirit above food, fashion, money and any other person or thing of this world! It is because we do not have such a passion to live in God's perfect will, that we take sin so lightly. Holiness is not the major passion of most Christians; hence they miss this fellowship. You and I need to do away with impurity and fellowship with the Father constantly. The main reason why Jesus always withdrew himself to solitary places was always to seek fellowship with God before appearing before men. Mary sought fellowship with Jesus while Martha sought to serve Him. And Jesus rebuked Martha saying that what

Mary chose was the first thing that matter (Luke 10:42). It is holiness that makes our service effective.

Be filled with love and compassion

I have mentioned that the heart of compassion is very important to receiving this baptism. This is simply because; the power is not for fun. The point here again in Luke 11is that you must, first of all, have *compassion and a burden* for the needy people you encounter. What comes to your heart when you see people afflicted with sickness, poverty, injustice, ignorance, marginalized or oppressed? Then you must recognize that only God can give you what is required to meet these needs. So, you must seek God first for His power. If your calling is to preach the word, then ask God first of all to give you a love and compassion for those you have to preach to. Then keep asking Him for the anointing and revelation of the Spirit for a specific word to meet their need. We can ask God in the same way if we have to pray for someone's healing or we have to cast out a demon from someone. You are not called to serve everyone in the whole wide world, but only those whom God sends to your way or send you to. This man did not want bread for all the hungry people in the countryside, but only for the one person who came to him. That needy person could be your son, daughter, congregation or even your neighbor. The need may be physical or spiritual. Jesus said that everyone who asks and knocks (like this man did) will get whatever he asks for (verses 9, 10). But those who knock only two or three times and give up will receive nothing. The same principle of prayer is taught in Luke 18:1ff.

Hence, even though your spirit man hates sins with all passion, yet the love of Christ will be shed in your heart for everybody regardless of the color, ethnicity, gender or nationality. You cannot be filled, immersed, or baptized in the Holy Spirit and be a hater. You cannot go on hating people just because they have views that are different from yours. Everyone does not need to agree with your point of view before you love them. *"For in Christ Jesus neither circumcision nor uncircumcision avails anything, but faith working through love"* (Gal 5:6).

In the Aaronic priesthood, God made it as an ordinance for the priest to always write the list of the tribes of Israel on the robe a priest wore as he appeared before the Lord to make atonement for them (Exodus 28: 21). If you have the people of God in your heart, God will always give you word for them. I remember this incident during the time of COVID-19 as an international student. I always worked for 20 hrs. per week (with $10 per hour). Despite the fact that my income per month is far away from meeting our monthly bills, yet there a certain percentage of our meager income that Peace and I normally send home for the hungry people around us who depend on us to survive. At a point in time, the pressure upon us from home became escalated and we sought the face of the Lord in prayers to provide. Few days later, a friend called us if we have hungry people around us. We answered yes affirmatively. The same person said, 'I have a gift of $500 for you to help those needy ones. "If you have it in your heart, the Lord will place it in your hand." (I share this testimony above with all humility). In the same way, when you have a heart of compassion, for the people, God will always release his power upon you to meet both their physical and spiritual needs.

Having the heart of service

And being found in appearance as a man, he humbled himself by becoming obedient to death—even death on a cross! (Philip 2: 8). Having the attitude of servanthood aligns you to receive the baptism. God does not empower us so that we can be served, but He empowers us for us to serve. You have to be at the low level of the spiritual waterfall for you to be immersed. A lot of people have fallen victim of using the anointing of the Holy Spirit to build empire for themselves. By this, they pollute themselves and also pollute their giftings. Are you seeking for this power primarily to serve with humility within the body of Christ, or you want to be famous and make men to serve you? *Jesus called them together and said, "You know that the rulers of the Gentiles lord it over them, and their high officials exercise authority over them. Not so with you. Instead, whoever wants to become great among you must be your servant, and whoever wants to be first must be your slave— just as the Son of Man did not come to be served, but to serve, and to give his life as a ransom for many"* (Matt 20: 25-28). Remember, Jesus humbled himself to serve before he was exalted by the Father. (Philip 2: 8)

Seeking Glory for God

Ultimately, God anoints us with power so that our deeds will bring glory to His name. Be careful if you are becoming more popular than Jesus among the people of your congregation. Do not point yourself to the people, rather point people to Jesus Christ the bridegroom. Stop taking away the bride of Jesus from him—it is dangerous. *And I will do whatever you ask in my name, so that the Father may be glorified in the Son* (John 14: 13). The cry of the early believers as seen in their prayers for revival was that God's

198

name be glorified among the heathens. *"And now, Lord, behold their threatenings: and grant unto thy servants, that with all boldness they may speak thy word, by stretching forth thine hand to heal; and that signs and wonders may be done by the name of thy holy child Jesus. And when they had prayed, the place was shaken where they were assembled together; and they were all filled with the Holy Ghost, and they spake the word of God with boldness"* (Acts 4: 29-31). If you are using the power of God upon you to seek glory for yourself, you may eventually ruin yourself someday. But if you are passionately seeking for God's name alone to be glorified in the place you are, then, you are set for the endowment of power.

Three stages of encounter with the Holy Spirit

As I study the teaching of Jesus Christ, from my own careful examination, there seems to be three stages of experience anyone can encounter with the Holy Spirit. Permit me to explain this in the analogy below. First, at the point of conversion or regeneration, you are reborn of the Holy Spirit and water. According to the word of Jesus Christ ". . . *Very truly I tell you, no one can enter the kingdom of God unless they are born of water and the Spirit* (John 3:5). The psalmist in his prophetic declaration called this rebirth with Spirit and water as the 'cup of salvation.' *"I will take the cup of salvation, and call upon the name of the LORD"* (Psalm 116:13). I compare this first stage like being filled with a cup of water of the Spirit. At this point, you are not totally satisfied yet. There are yearnings and quests in your heart to know more about this new life. From here you can move to the second stage of encounter with the Holy Spirit, depending on your yielding. At the second encounter, this cup of water of the Holy Spirit becomes a 'well or a spring' of living spring. To this, Jesus said; *"Jesus answered, "Everyone who drinks this water will be thirsty again, but whoever drinks the water I give them will never thirst. Indeed, the water I give them will become in them a spring of water welling up to eternal life"* (John 4:13-14). The second stage of encounter with the Holy Spirit meets all your personal spiritual needs; the yoke of sins—lusts, anger, bitterness, jealousy, unforgiveness etc., is completely broken, and you are able to serve the living God. But from here, we can still move as well to the next stage.

At the third stage, you are fully immersed in the ocean of the Spirit and it is at this stage your life begins to impact everyone around you and anyone you come in contact with. The Scripture affirms; "On the last and greatest day of the festival, Jesus stood and said in a loud voice, let anyone who is thirsty come to me and drink.

Whoever believes in me, as Scripture has said, rivers of living water will flow from within them. By this he meant the Spirit, whom those who believed in him were later to receive. Up to that time the Spirit had not been given, since Jesus had not yet been glorified" (John 7:37-39).

How do we get to the second and third stage? We get there by diligent seeking and a thirsting heart. Hear what the scripture say, *"You will seek me and find me when you seek me with all your heart"* (Jeremiah 29:13); *"In the last day, that great day of the feast, Jesus stood and cried, saying, if any man thirst, let him come unto me, and drink"* (John 7:37); But without faith it is impossible to please him: for he that cometh to God must believe that he is, and that he is a rewarder of them that diligently seek him (Hebrews 11:6). Until you become an addicted seeker, who is hungry and thirsty to be filled with the power of the Holy Spirit, you may just remain as casual or nominal Christians all the days of your life. *"And ye shall seek me, and find me, when ye shall search for me with all your heart"* (Jer 29: 13). A half-hearted believer or seeker cannot enjoy the fullness of God presence and power.

Chapter 14

The Deception of Miracles, Signs and Wonders

Many will say to me on that day, 'Lord, Lord, did we not prophesy in your name and in your name drive out demons and in your name perform many miracles?' Then I will tell them plainly, 'I never knew you. Away from me, you evildoers! (Matt 7: 22-23)

The fact that there is the fake of a thing is a proof that there is an original of it. Hence, the fact that there are lot of fake miracle workers today is never a justifiable ground to deny the miraculous act of God through many of his servants till date. Right from the beginning till now, Jesus Christ is still confirming the gospel with signs and wonders as he pleases. Regardless of your position about signs and wonders today, Jesus Christ is the same, yesterday, today and forever. No one can cage the operation of the Holy Spirit in a box.

The End does not justify the means

I have heard severally from different men of God the slogan 'results silence the critics. Hence, if it works, it is approved.' But the fact that someone claim to perform miracle in the Name of Christ does not mean that God approves his life. Many modern church leaders focus on how to make Christianity become more marketable. They place more emphasis on packaging the gospel in a more attractive way. Jared C. Wilson has a good description for this when he writes on attractional churches. According to Jared, the term "attractional" refers to "a way of doing church ministry whose primary purpose is to make Christianity appealing."[1] As a matter of fact, the attractional model is not just a matter of mere style; rather, it has become a paradigm. Church leaders are now adopting the modus operandi of pragmatism and consumerism[2] by redirecting people attention to miracles, signs and wonders instead of making people focus on Christ. The ideologies behind these seem to fit into Wilson's description:

> "We will do whatever it takes to get people in the door," I often hear pastors say. "We just want them to be able to hear the message of Jesus." That latter motivation is wonderful, but the problem is that "doing whatever it takes to get people in the door" can replace or undercut what we want them to be attracted to. Whatever you win people with is what you win them to. The best motives in the world cannot sanctify unbiblical methods.[3]

---

[1] Jared C. Wilson, *The Gospel-Driven Church: Uniting Church-Growth with the Metrics of Grace* (Grand Rapids: Zondervan, 2019), 24.

[2] "Pragmatism" has to do with "If it works, then work it." In this ideology, the end always justifies the means. In January 2020, I interviewed a member of well know church in Africa concerning the signs and wonders In part of his response, the man said, "My Papa use to say, 'only a fool will deny the proof." Statement like this is highly misleading. On the other hand, "consumerism" is a business term with an ideology of trying to satisfy the desire of the consumers (or customers) at all costs.

[3] Wilson, *The Gospel-Driven Church*, 24.

Hence, to keep their converts in their churches, today's church founders must continue to focus members' attention on miracles, signs and wonders. Nevertheless, if a method does not depend on the genuine leading of the Holy Spirit, then adopting pragmatism in order to keep followers remains awkward. Whatever one's approach to evangelism and church growth is, redirecting people to anything (or anyone) other than Jesus jeopardizes the real gospel.

A Lesson from Moses, Aaron, and the Israelites

At the Desert called Zin, when Moses hit the Rock instead of speaking to the Rock, water did not just sprinkle out from the rock, but gushed out to satisfy the thirst of over a million of the people of Israel (besides their livestock) who were so famished to the point of cursing God. Apart from disobeying the instruction of God by striking the rock twice, Moses seemed to give the credit to himself and his brother for that great act of God to provide water in the wilderness. Moses' word revealed this ego when he said, "*You rebels, SHALL WE bring you water out of this rock?*" (Number 20:10). Instead of speaking to the Rock as God commanded, Moses projected himself as the one doing the miracle. God was so displeased with Moses and Aaron over this, but water gushed out anyway. They were able to provide water abundantly in a miraculous way for the people, but God was no longer in it. That very day, their disengagement from ministry was sealed by God but their followers did not know (Number 20:12).

Even though God still went ahead to use them in some great ways for His people, Israel, yet God was already done with them, working out their exit. Friends, it is not everything that seems to work that has God's approval in it. It is not everything 'that works' that has been commanded by God. That God brought out water from the rocks did not mean Moses' life or action was pleasing to God. It only meant God was keen on meeting the needs of the people. On the other hand, even the Israelites, who were the recipients of several miracles from God, was under God's wrath. *"For forty years I was angry with that generation; I said, 'They are a people whose hearts go astray, and they have not known my ways"* (Ps 95: 10). According to this scripture, for forty years—meaning right from the year one that the Israelites left Egypt, God was not happy with them because, right from the very first day they were coming out of Egypt, God had seen their heart of unbelief. Hence, that someone is used by God to perform miracles or that someone receives miracle from God is never a proof of God's approval (Matt 7: 21f).

Whenever I hear somebody saying "the principle works" to connote he is doing it right or that he is approved of God, I always pause to think twice. Idols worshippers who are doing some magic also have proofs to back up their claims— "it works!" Stop following people that say their principles work. There are many things that work but have no God's signet ring on them. That someone has a proof is never enough evidence that his life or ministry is approved by God. Be careful! There are many modernized herbalists and idol worshippers in churches today who are in sheep's clothing deceiving gullible minds. Watch out for the fruit of their holy lives and test all spirits. Do not be deceived by charismatic giftings. Till date, it is *"An evil and adulterous generation seeks after a sign"* (Matthew 12:39-40). Again, if you are projecting yourself instead of projecting Christ, you might just be awaiting disengagement like Moses. Moses never knew that the Rock he struck twice with the rod was Christ (1Cor.10:4). Note again, miracle does not make any prophet or preacher qualified before God as an approved man. Samson, after sleeping with harlot for a whole night still went and carried a whole city gate and threw it a yonder to the Kidron valley (Judges 16). Many people have polluted the giftings of God upon their lives. There are men who will sleep in hotels with women, yet still go on stage the following day to see visions, prophesy and perform some 'acrobatics' in the name of miracles, signs and wonders. The most amazing thing is that in their delusion, the vulnerable audience still hail them and regard them as men of God. For a good 13 years, king Saul had been replaced with David; heaven had terminated king Saul's duty, yet he remained on the throne leading the Israelite army in battle. But since the day David was anointed with oil, Saul had ceased to be king in God's calendar (1 Samuel 16). Do not let God replace or displace you.

Remember again, Satan can manipulate people to perform miracles. This was the first temptation he pushed toward Jesus—he wanted Jesus to turn stone into bread if Jesus was really a Son of God (Matt 4:1-4). Inferentially, we can deduce that not every miracle today comes from God; Satan can manipulate people to perform miracle to boost their ego and pride. When miracle workers of today perform miracles after demanding for money, and when those miracles make people to turn attention to them (instead of looking unto Jesus), to give them honor, and to make them become famous like the movie's stars of the world; you can be pretty sure that most of such miracles are motivated by the devil—not Christ.

These are part of the reasons why the recipients of such miracles in few days' return back to their former situations; and some even become worst.

Chapter 15

The Parable of Another Jesus

For as I have often told you before, and now say
again even with tears: Many live as enemies of the
cross of Christ. Their end is destruction, their god
is their belly, and their glory is in their shame.
Their minds are set on earthly things
(Philp 3: 18-19)

I got this as a devotional email from Zac Poonen, and with

permission, I am devoting this chapter to the message. It really will

bless your spirit as it does to mine.

Another Jesus and His Ministry

"You seem so gullible: You believe whatever
*anyone tells you even if he is preaching **another***
***Jesus** than the One we preach" (2 Cor.11:4 –*
Living Bible).

Imagine that you were in Palestine nearly 2000 years ago

and that you heard of the ministry of someone called *"Jesus of*

Nazareth" who was healing the sick. Not having seen Him yourself,

you are delighted when you come across a large crowd attending a

healing meeting in Jerusalem, with someone called `Jesus' as the

speaker. *"The Word of God gives a clear light for all who desire it*

in these last days."

As you draw nearer, you find that up on the platform, along

with ' `Jesus' the speaker, Pilate and Herod, and Annas and Caiaphas are also seated. `Jesus' then comes forward and addresses the crowd saying how honored they all should feel that day because the two greatest secular rulers of Palestine, "the most honorable Herod and Pilate had graciously come to honor the meeting with their presence". And not only that, but "two great men of God, the Right Reverend Annas and Caiaphas were also there to bless the gathering." Having spoken these words of introduction, `Jesus' then invites Herod and Pilate to inaugurate the meeting and to speak a few words. Herod and Pilate both praise `Jesus' and say what a lot of good he is doing to the community by his ministry and that he deserves the support of all the people. The Right Reverend Annas and Caiaphas are then invited by `Jesus' to say a few words and to "open in prayer". They also praise `Jesus' highly and invite all the people in their denomination to support `Jesus's ministry wholeheartedly.

Then `Jesus' invites Judas Iscariot to say a few words about the financial needs of the ministry. Judas speaks about the tens of thousands of dollars needed to meet all the needs of the ministry. He states that 'forms' are available with the ushers for those who contribute more than 1000 dollars saying that `Jesus' has promised to pray special prayers for such people (it does not matter whether they are believers or unbelievers – all the rich are welcome and the richer the better!). Herod then gets up and offers to give a tax deduction to all those who contribute to this ministry. The collection is then taken. Then *'Jesus'* gives a brief message, demonstrates a few of his miraculous powers that astound the simple people, and "heals" a few sick people [and make some to fall down under the anointing. Then Peter came on stage to make announcement about the available mantle—handkerchief, anointing oil, anointing bottle water, anointing wrist bands with 'Jesus' photo on them etc, for sale with the ushers. And then before anyone can meet him, he rushes off with Herod, Pilate, Annas, Caiaphas and Judas Iscariot (and the bags of money) in the royal Roman chariot to the archbishop's palace in central Jerusalem to feast with them. Somehow, at the end of all this, even though you are only a new convert, with little discernment and experience, you still feel a bit uneasy. All that you saw does not seem to fit in with the accounts that you had heard about Jesus from some of His apostles like Matthew, Peter and John. Satan, however, is nearby to whisper in your ears, "It is written, *'Do not judge'*" (Matt. 7:1). But you tell him, "It is also written, *'Do not believe every spirit, but test the spirits to see whether they are from God, because many false prophets have gone out into the world'*" (1

211

John 4:1). Finally, you come to a definite conclusion: "This is not the Jesus that I heard about. This is certainly *"another Jesus."* And you are right. It was another `Jesus'. How did you come to that conclusion? Because the anointing within you told you the following facts (1 John 2:19,20,27):

- The real Jesus would not seek any sponsorship from secular rulers or any recommendation from unconverted religious heads for His ministry. Neither would He flatter any of them. When a bishop once came to Jesus, He told him that he needed to be born again (Jn. 3:1-10). Jesus called King Herod 'a fox' (Lk. 13:31, 32) and even refused to talk to him when He met him (Lk. 23:8,9).

- The real Jesus would never ask anyone for money – not even for His ministry. He made His needs known only to His Father. The Father would then move people or even a fish (in one instance) to supply Jesus' need (Lk. 8:1-3; Matt. 17:27).

- The real Jesus would never 'sell' His prayers for any price. Simon the Samaritan magician once offered money for Peter's prayers and Peter rebuked him for such wickedness as to imagine that a divine gift could be bought with money (Acts 8:18-23). Simon repented immediately. But his unrepentant followers have been many through the centuries. Those who claim to be the successors of Peter however still sell their prayers for money. Martin Luther stood against such wickedness in his day, like Peter. But some of the successors of Luther (today's Protestants) have started selling their 'prayers' and their 'prophecies' for cash; and alas, many like Simon are willing to pay for them!

- Jesus specifically warned us that in the last days, deception would be so subtle that even the elect would almost be deceived - particularly through signs and wonders (Matt

212

24:24). If there is any ministry that the elect are to beware of and examine most carefully today, it is the 'sign and wonder' ministry. Jesus still does miracles and heals the sick through genuine gifts of the Holy Spirit. But not everything that goes by Jesus' name is genuine.

Jesus told us not to believe it when people say that He came *physically* to their rooms (See Matt. 24:26). Our Lord has promised to be with us (in His Spirit) until the end of the age, but we will see Him *physically* only when He returns in glory. The resurrected body of Jesus has never left the right hand of the Father in all these (more than 1900) years since His ascension. Paul and Stephen saw Him only there (Acts 7:55; 9:3). Even John did not see Jesus' *physical* body on Patmos but only symbols representing Jesus (Rev. 1:13-16). When Jesus does leave heaven finally, it will be only for His second coming to earth. Therefore, when they say today that He came *physically* to their rooms, *"do not believe them."* Living in the midst of gullible believers, we must not remain without discernment. The Word of God gives a clear light for all who desire it in these last days. If we follow that light alone, we will never be deceived.[1]

---

[1] Poonen, devotional email message title "Another 'Jesus' And His Ministry 23 July 2017

Chapter 16

Abuse of the Spiritual Power

*". . . For such people are not serving our Lord
Christ, but their own appetites. By smooth talk and
flattery, they deceive the minds of naive people
(Rom 16: 17-18)*

Seeking the power for self-aggrandizement

In Luke 4:4, we read that after Jesus was tempted, he returned in the power of the Spirit to preach. Overcoming temptation always enables us to minister God's word with power. In the synagogue in Nazareth, Jesus read Isaiah 61: 1-2 (cf Lk 4: 17-21) and said that the prophecy was now fulfilled. The Spirit of God anointed him to bless others—to preach the gospel to others, to release others from prison, to open the eyes of others, and to set other free. Every result of the anointing was for others. The fruit of the Spirit is for ourselves—love, joy, peace, long suffering, gentleness, goodness, faithfulness, meekness and self-control. But the gifts of the Spirit are all for others. If God gives you the gift of preaching or healing, it is to bless others with—and not for you to make money or get honor for yourself. If you use a gift of the Spirit for yourself, you will only build Babylon with it—and not the true church of Christ.

Do not make your influence as tool for manipulations

Another danger is when you start using the power of God in seeking man's praise. Jesus once said; '*I do not receive praise or testimony from men; I do not receive glory from men*' (John 5:34, 41). Jesus is satisfied with the testimony of his Father about him, man's testimony counts to nothing before him. The desire to receive plastic praise from people has hindered many from having genuine and living faith. Be careful when men start to sing your praises. Make a decision today never to seek for honor from any mortal man. When you allow the gift of God to turn you into a 'deity' or 'god'— and you allow yourself to be idolized, you are at the brim of destruction. Whenever pride and ego consume you so much that you can no longer humble yourself, the power you are wielding is satanic. Humility comes with the power, genuine power of the Holy Spirit. There are so many charismatic leaders today who have charisma but without godly character. What is the essence of have the power of the Holy Spirit without the character of the Holy Spirit? If you enjoy sinning, taking the advantage of the weak-willed followers by assaulting them sexually under the disguise that you carry power of the Spirit, you are of the 'evil one.' You need to repent! The rate of sexual immoralities among the so-called people who claim to have the operation of sign gifts is becoming an embarrassment to the symbol of Christianity. You cannot know a true man of God by the giftings but by the fruit – fruit, not miracles (Matt 7: 15-21).

Dividing a peaceful church

The baptism of the Holy Spirit that some young people of our generation claim to have is not but a gift of rebellion from the devil. For more than ten years now, I have been a pastor in a church-denomination that does not permit public display of tongues. The church follows strictly the teaching of Paul about the operation of spiritual gifts in the church as seen in 1 Cor. 14. I have never for once jumped on the pulpit to start speaking in tongues, and that does not stop God from working or saving souls. Interestingly too, throughout all the years of his public ministry, we never see Jesus, not even for once coming into the Temple or any synagogue to start speaking in tongues so as to prove that he was more spiritual than the high priest and the rabbi of his days. The spirit of a prophet is subject to the prophet (1 Cor 14: 32). However, when I am alone in my privacy, I speak as the Holy Spirit brings the utterances. Do not rebel against the elders and pastors of your church with any gift the Spirit gives you. Many young ones are roaming about today with rebellious spirits which they call 'spiritual gifts,' and many of them do not last long on the spiritual journey.

Syncretism and Demonic Practices

There are pseudo-manifestations of spiritual powers today under the disguise of the anointing of the Holy Spirit. Many are displaying voodoo power, magical practices, the practice of witchcraft and the likes claiming they are under the power of the Holy Spirit. The powers which some of today's miracle workers are wielding come from demonic sources. In most part of Africa, today's modern Christianity is nothing but mingling the practice of Christianity with some elements in the African Traditional Religions. I elaborated on these syncretic practices in my book, "Nigerian Neo-Pentecostals: A Glimpse to African Modern Christianity." Some have lost their connection with the Holy Spirit, but to continue to keep themselves relevant to their follower; they turn to diabolical powers. This is why it important to seek for the fruit of Christlikeness in any professing minister of the gospel than focusing on the gifts of the Spirit (Matt 7:13-20; Gal. 5:21-24)

Building family Empire

It baffles to see how church business has graduated to family business affair. The man is the general overseer, the wife is the

217

assistant and the children manage the church finances according to the directives received from the ('G.O'). The in-laws too handle some other sensitive positions in the ministries. As the father age in ministry, he prepares to hand over to his son. We have seen cases of a mother and son fighting over who should take over as leader of the church/ministry after the demise of the father. The mother wants to be the general overseer; the son wants to be as well. These types of denominations are purely private family business affair. Innocent members are exploited to make the family extremely rich with extravagant lifestyles. These pastors cannot handover to different committed followers who do not belong to their families. We read of Moses who handed over to a different Joshua who had no family relational link to Moses.

Again, there are several one-man-show kinds of ministries among today's modern preachers. I know a pastor in Nigeria that used to run more than six services on Sundays. In all of these services, he wouldn't allow any of the pastors under him to preach or teach except himself, his wife, his spiritual father(s) who visited by invitations, and some foreign preachers during the church special programs, are the only one qualified to preach. Many Nigerian Neo-Pentecostal pastors do not trust people around them. As a result of lack of rest, a G.O once collapsed and was rushed to foreign country for treatment only for the congregation to be told that the man is enjoying his vacation. They will not say their pastor is sick, because 'it is almost a taboo to say a man of such anointing is sick.'

Measuring Anointing of the Holy Spirit with Material Prosperity

Material prosperity will not lead anyone to heaven nor is it the way to heaven. Freedom from sins is the way to heaven. This is the first promise in the new covenant (Matt. 1:21). The prophetic voices that expose sins in the innermost places are lacking in Christendom today. Many thought that the prophetic ministry in the church is all about predicting the future. The biblical prophetic ministry is exposing and rebuking hidden sins through the anointing of the Holy Spirit and the undiluted truth of God's word. This is what always lead people to genuine repentance from sins that are destroying them (1 Cor 14: 24-25). It is so pathetic how many today measure success in ministry with material accumulation on earth.

Chapter 17

Exploitation of Unbelievers in the name of Anointing

"But godliness with contentment is great gain" (1
Timo 6: 6)

I will want all the gospel preachers to take caution on this
very particular matter.

> *A good man leaves an inheritance to his children's children:*
> *and the wealth of the sinner is laid up for the just* (Proverb
> 13:22).

This very common Old Testament scriptural text has been severally
misinterpreted out of context by many greedy preachers to
shamelessly rake out money and other materials from the
unbelievers. The second text that is always quoted out of context
read as,

> *And I will make the Egyptians favorably disposed toward*
> *this people, so that when you leave you will not go empty-*
> *handed. Every woman is to ask her neighbor and any woman*
> *living in her house for articles of silver and gold and for*
> *clothing, which you will put on your sons and daughters.*
> *And so you will plunder the Egyptians.......... The Israelites*
> *did as Moses instructed and asked the Egyptians for articles*
> *of silver and gold and for clothing. The LORD had made the*
> *Egyptians favorably disposed toward the people, and they*
> *gave them what they asked for; so they plundered the*
> *Egyptians* (Exodus 3:21-22; 12:35-36).

Do you remember that for over four hundred years the
Israelites served the Egyptians under hard labor without payment?

The Egyptians task masters made life tough for the Israelites. God is a God of justice, and He simply made the Egyptians to pay all the wages of the Israelites for all these years of forceful servitudes. Hence, to be teaching your congregation to go and reap where they have not sown with the heart of covetousness for materialism is another way of teaching them how to become armed robbers. Why don't you teach them how to be creative to solve societal challenges instead of all those forms of mediocrity prayers that center upon taking what does not belong to you by force?

In regard to coveting unbelievers' silver and gold, let learn what the Bible has to say.

Abraham refused to covet the riches of unbelieving king of Sodom

> *But Abram said to the king of Sodom, "With raised hand I have sworn an oath to the LORD, God Most High, Creator of heaven and earth, that **I will accept nothing belonging to you**, not even a thread or the strap of a sandal, **so that you will never be able to say, 'I made Abram rich.** 'I will accept nothing but what my men have eaten and the share that belongs to the men who went with me...* (Genesis 14:22-24).

Moses never covets anyone animals or material property

> *Then Moses became very angry and said to the LORD, "Do not accept their offering. I have not taken so much as a donkey from them, nor have I wronged any of them* (Numbers 16: 15)

Prophet Samuel laid down a good example

I have been your leader from my youth until this day. Here I stand. Testify against me in the presence of the LORD and his anointed. Whose ox have I taken? Whose donkey have I taken? Whom have I cheated? Whom have I oppressed? From whose hand have I accepted a bribe to make me shut my eyes? If I have done any of these things, I will make it right. You have not cheated or oppressed us," they replied. "You have not taken anything from anyone's hand. "Samuel said to them, "The LORD is witness against you, and also his anointed is witness this day, that you have not found anything in my hand (1 Samuel 12:2b-5)

Prophet Elisha rejected Naaman gifts after healing him

Then Naaman and all his attendants went back to the man of God. He stood before him and said, "Now I know that there is no God in all the world except in Israel. So please accept a gift from your servant. "The prophet answered, **"As surely as the LORD lives, whom I serve, I will not accept a thing."** *And even though Naaman urged him, he refused* (2 Kings 5:15-16).

Daniel rejected Belteshazzar gifts after interpreting the mysterious handwriting on the wall

King Belteshazzar said to Daniel.... Now I have heard that you are able to give interpretations and to solve difficult problems. If you can read this writing and tell me what it means, you will be clothed in purple and have a gold chain placed around your neck, and you will be made the third highest ruler in the kingdom." Then Daniel answered the king, "You may keep your gifts for yourself and give your rewards to someone else. Nevertheless, I will read the writing for the king and tell him what it means (Daniel 5:16-17).

Peter rejected the money of Simon the Sorcerer

When Simon saw that the Spirit was given at the laying on of the apostles' hands, he offered them money and said, "Give me also this ability so that everyone on whom I lay my hands may receive the Holy Spirit." Peter answered: "May your money perish with you, because you thought you could buy the gift of God with money! You have no part or share in this ministry, because your heart is not right before God. Repent of this wickedness and pray to the Lord in the hope that he may forgive you for having such a thought in your heart. For I see that you are full of bitterness and captive to sin (Acts 8:18-23)

Apostle Paul had a contentment spirit

I have not coveted anyone's silver or gold or clothing. You yourselves know that these hands of mine have supplied my own needs and the needs of my companions (Acts 20:33-34)

They went out in Christ name not collecting anything from pagans

It was for the sake of the Name (of Christ) that they went out, receiving no help from the pagans. We ought therefore to show hospitality to such people so that we may work together for the truth (3John 7-8).

In fact, one of the ways to identify false prophet in the early church is whenever anyone who called himself a preacher of the gospel asked for money. By this, people quickly know that he is a wolf in sheep's clothing.

Jesus Christ refused to bow for the Devil in exchange for the riches of this world

Again, the devil took him to a very high mountain and showed him all the kingdoms of the world and their splendor. "All this I will give you," he said, "if you will bow down and worship me." Jesus said to him, "Away from me, Satan! For it is written: 'Worship the Lord your God, and serve him only (Matthew 4:8-10).

There are many preachers, evangelists and church leaders that are bowing to the devil and unbelievers today just to make themselves rich at all cost. I never dispute the fact that God can use anything or anyone to meet your need by His Own sovereign will. But if you greedily go after unbelievers' silvers and gold, you are only using God's name to rob and dupe people. When a drug dealer, a womanizer, an occultist and their likes become the one sponsoring your evangelistic ministry or your television programs as preacher, then you are a compromiser.

We are no longer seeing men of God like Prophet Samuel who on his farewell speech to the Israelites confidently stood up to say;

Samuel said to all Israel, "I have listened to everything you said to me and have set a king over you. Now you have a king as your leader. As for me, I am old and gray, and my sons are here with you. I have been your leader from my youth until this day. Here I stand. Testify against me in the presence of the LORD and his anointed. Whose ox have I taken? Whose donkey have I taken? Whom have I cheated? Whom have I oppressed? From whose hand have I accepted a bribe to make me shut my eyes? If I have done any of these things, I will make it right." "You have not cheated or oppressed us," they replied. "You have not taken anything from anyone's hand." Samuel said to them, "The LORD is witness against you, and also his anointed is witness this day, that you have not found anything in my hand. "He is witness," they said (1Samuel 12:1-5).

In the same manner, Apostle Paul made his own declaration to the Corinthians church.

> *For it seems to me that God has put us apostles on display at the end of the procession, like those condemned to die in the arena. We have been made a spectacle to the whole universe, to angels as well as to human beings. We are fools for Christ, but you are so wise in Christ! We are weak, but you are strong! You are honored, we are dishonored. To this very hour we go hungry and thirsty, we are in rags, we are brutally treated, we are homeless. We work hard with our own hands. When we are cursed, we bless; when we are persecuted, we endure it; when we are slandered, we answer kindly. We have become the scum of the earth, the garbage of the world—right up to this moment* (1 Corinthians 4: 9-13).

> *If we have sown spiritual seed among you, is it too much if we reap a material harvest from you? If others have this right of support from you, shouldn't we have it all the more?* **But we did not use this right. On the contrary, we put up with anything rather than hinder the gospel of Christ. Don't** *you know that those who serve in the temple get their food from the temple, and that those who serve at the altar share in what is offered on the altar? In the same way, the Lord has commanded that those who preach the gospel should receive their living from the gospel. But I have not used any of these rights.* **And I am not writing this in the hope that you will do such things for me, for I would rather die than allow anyone to deprive me of this boast.** *For when I preach the gospel, I cannot boast, since I am compelled to preach. Woe to me if I do not preach the gospel! If I preach voluntarily, I have a reward; if not voluntarily, I am simply discharging the trust committed to me. What then is my reward? Just this:* **that in preaching the gospel I may offer it free of charge, and so not make full use of my rights as a preacher of the gospel** (1 Corinthians 9:11-18).

> *Whatever anyone else dares to boast about—I am speaking as a fool—I also dare to boast about. Are they Hebrews? So am I. Are they Israelites? So am I. Are they Abraham's*

*descendants? So am I. Are they servants of Christ? (I am out of my mind to talk like this.) I am more. I have worked much harder, **been in prison more frequently, been flogged more severely, and been exposed to death again and again. Five times I received from the Jews the forty lashes minus one. Three times I was beaten with rods, once I was pelted with stones, three times I was shipwrecked, I spent a night and a day in the open sea,** I have been constantly on the move. I have been in danger from rivers, in danger from bandits, in danger from my fellow Jews, in danger from Gentiles; in danger in the city, in danger in the country, in danger at sea; and in danger from false believers. I have labored and toiled and have often gone without sleep; **I have known hunger and thirst and have often gone without food; I have been cold and naked.** Besides everything else, I face daily the pressure of my concern for all the churches. Who is weak, and I do not feel weak? Who is led into sin, and I do not inwardly burn? If I must boast, I will boast of the things that show my weakness. The God and Father of the Lord Jesus, who is to be praised forever, knows that I am not lying. In Damascus the governor under King Aretas had the city of the Damascenes guarded in order to arrest me. But I was lowered in a basket from a window in the wall and slipped through his hands* (2 Corinthians 11: 22-33).

It is so pathetic how many preachers today have seen godliness as a doorway to financial gains. The Scripture really warns against this.

*These are the things you are to teach and insist on. If anyone teaches otherwise and does not agree to the sound instruction of our Lord Jesus Christ and to godly teaching, they are conceited and understand nothing. They have an unhealthy interest in controversies and quarrels about words that result in envy, strife, malicious talk, evil suspicions and constant friction between people of corrupt mind, **who have been robbed of the truth and who think that godliness is a means to financial gain*** (1 Timothy 6:2-5).

One Neo-Pentecostal pastor had once preached that if you are broke financially as Christian, then you need to check your spiritual life. Some are of the opinion that it is a taboo to be poor as Christian. What about Paul that went about saying; *I have known hunger and thirst and have often gone without food; I have been cold and naked*? Frankly speaking, today, no any gospel preacher, apostles, man of God, pastor or evangelist want to pass through these kind of suffering again. Every one of us wants to ride the latest car in town, we want to live in the best house, we want to enjoy the latest technologies, and we want to be the richest pastor in town. Everybody wants to dwell in comfort zone as we do God's works. What about all the believers in the early church that died without any personal property monetary assets to point to? Just as poverty is never a sign of righteousness, in the same way, materialism is never a sign of spirituality. Or else we would have asked, what about non-Christians that are extremely rich in silver, gold and with sound health? Indeed, *godliness with contentment is a great gain* (1 Timothy 6:6).

To the Ephesians church Paul said;

I have not coveted anyone's silver or gold or clothing. You yourselves know that these hands of mine have supplied my own needs and the needs of my companions. In everything I did, I showed you that by this kind of hard work we must help the weak, remembering the words the Lord Jesus himself said: 'It is more blessed to give than to receive (Acts 20:33-35).

God's servants of old never extort people to make themselves wealthy out of the gospel. It is very easy to extort people today in the name of the gospel. For example, if you have a crowd of 1million at a sitting, it is a matter of passing offering basket. If everyone gives offering of $2 each, that will be a total of $2million. But that is not the style of Jesus. Any time the multitude of crowd followed him, he would always teach them, feed them and let them go free of charge without even raising offering for His next missions' trip. **This is a hard teaching, right**? If there is a genuine need for the gospel, make it known to the people of God (not the sinners that you are preaching to). Again, do not gather the collections from God's people for your personal luxury and greed. ***Do not covet anyone's silver or gold or clothing.*** We really need the help of God so that we will not be serving money (mammon) while erroneously thinking we are working for God. There are too many out there today claiming to be working for God but whose stomach is their god.

For, as I have often told you before and now tell you again even with tears, many live as enemies of the cross of Christ. Their destiny is destruction, their god is their stomach, and their glory is in their shame. Their mind is set on earthly

228

things. But our citizenship is in heaven (Philippians 3: 18-20).

We need to learn from the contemporary heroes and heroines of faith as well. Billy Graham is one of the men God has tremendously used in this generation. His ministry has pulled several millions of crowds. History and acquaintances, have it that, he used all gains in the sale of his productions purely on the gospel. No luxury, no accumulation of money in his personal bank account, no building or buying of new houses. The same house he had when he got married in the 1950s is still the same house he retired to in the suburb of North Carolina. Remember the scripture that says; For they are traveling for the Lord, and they accept nothing from people who are not believers (3 John 1:7).

Stop Merchandizing the Gospel

When some pastors have prayed over objects like oil, handkerchiefs or prayer cloths, water (in the bottles), hand-bands, and the likes, those objects are then referred to as "mantles" which are made available for sale to the members. The mantles are seen as carriers of miracles, and they can be used for various miraculous activities as deemed fit. These types of men have twisted Act 19: 12 to suit their selfish ambitions. In most places, the mantles have turned to charm that some members hang on the walls, hide under

229

their beds, keep in handbags, attached to the body, and some put permanently in the offices and in the cars – all for the purpose of protection from enemies and favor from people. Several Pentecostal leaders have made their fortunes from these different mantles or prayer objects. There are some men of God who have 'miracle' wells or ponds. They claim that water fetched out from these wells will heal all manner of sicknesses and disease. A Nigerian prophet once claimed if you dip yourself in his pond, you will come out healed from all sicknesses. However, it will cost N50,000 (an average one-month wages) to enter the pond once. It is highly alarming how several people fall victims of all these gimmicks and have been duped by the so-called men of God. Stop merchandizing the gospel. When Jesus sent out his disciples on a mission's field, he said, *"Heal the sick, raise the dead, cleanse those who have leprosy, drive out demons. Freely you have received; freely give"* (Matt 10: 8).

Chapter18

Living in the Spirit

"For those who are led by the Spirit of God are the children of God" (Rom 8: 14)

As I have mentioned, when you are regenerated, you do not wait for many days to receive the Holy Spirit, he comes right there to dwell in you. That was why you were convicted of your sin, you acknowledged your helplessness, and you received Jesus as Lord and Savior. You cannot accept the invitation of Jesus without the Holy Spirit who quickens your spirit man to accept the righteousness of Jesus as gift. Your regeneration takes place by the work of the Holy Spirit, who immediately baptized you into the body of Christ and uniting you with other members of this body. Again, at conversion, the Spirit gives new spiritual life. Without the Spirit, you cannot belong to Christ (John 3:6; Rom 8:9). Through the Spirit, God adopts each believer as His child forever (Rom 8:14-16; Gal 4:6). God has set His seal of ownership on us and put His Spirit in our hearts as a deposit, guaranteeing what is to come (2 Cor 1:21-22; Eph 1:13-14).

But to be empowered by the Holy Spirit, sometimes it might be instant, or it may take days, weeks, months, or years. Nevertheless, if you really experience this power, you will know you have it. When were you filled with the Holy Spirit in power? Do away with empty church doctrine or powerless head knowledge that will hinder you from experiencing this power in your life. Water baptism takes place when you are immersed completely in the water. In the same way, the baptism of power comes by you being immersed in the Spirit. This baptism takes place when the Holy Spirit takes full control of your life. If the same Holy Spirit lives in us today, why are we not doing the same thing they did then? Why are we not sharing the gospel passionately?

When the Holy Spirit comes to indwell a person, he lives there forever (John14: 16). However, sin grieves the Holy Spirit (John 14:16; Eph 4:30). When we cling to sin, we lose the power, peace, love and joy of the Holy Spirit. The Spirit's sorrowful silence may even cause a believer to doubt their salvation. God may mercifully allow this sense of loss to continue until we repent. Praise God for the blood of Christ, which cleanses us from our sin.[1]

Nothing we do by human energy alone can please God (Rom 8:8). Do you serve Christ in your church or community? Do you try to lead your family to know and love Him? Are you attempting to succeed in your job or profession? Only through the Holy Spirit can

---

[1] "Preparing for Pentecost," BSF notes on Act 1 September 2019.

your work last to eternity. Without him, we can do nothing (John 15:5). Have you tried to retain control over your life? Will you stop now and submit consciously to the Holy Spirit and let him guide you.

The more the Holy Spirit controls your life, the more you will grow mand mature as a Christian. The opposite also holds true: the more you choose to live life on your own terms, the less spiritual power you will have. Your Christian life may be full of activity but with no results that last to eternity—no abiding fruit (John 15:16). If you want fruitful life, begin now to pray for humility to allow God's word to guide your thoughts, words, activities, and time. Will you ask God to control every part of your personality through his Spirit?[2]

Steps to a Spirit-filled Living

How then will I continue to live in the Spirit? In addition to the many factors that have been discussed in the previous chapters, I will itemize some key steps toward experiencing a continuous daily life of the Sprit.

Living a crucified life

Jesus once said, *"Verily, verily, I say unto you, except a corn of wheat fall into the ground and die, it abideth alone: but if it dies,*

---

[2] "Preparing for Pentecost," BSF notes on Act 1September 2019.

it bringeth forth much fruit" (John 12:24). There is a need of daily dying to self. "I die daily" (1 Cor 15:31). The Apostle Paul in the book of Galatians, made references to three different crucifixions that we need to experience. The first is the crucifixion of the old man. "I have been crucified with Christ and I no longer live, but Christ lives in me. The life I now live in the body, I live by faith in the Son of God, who loved me and gave himself for me" (Gal 2:20). The second is the crucifixion of the flesh and its sinful desires. "Those who belong to Christ Jesus have crucified the flesh with its passions and desires" (Gal 5: 24). The third is the crucifixion of the world to me, and I to the world. "May I never boast except in the cross of our Lord Jesus Christ, through which the world has been crucified to me, and I to the world" (Gal 6:14). This simply means that you and the world are no longer heading in the same direction, but in opposite direction (1 John 2:15-17; James 4:4). If your views, thinking and opinions in life go toward the same direction as people of the world, then you need to check yourself.

To be "filled" with the Spirit (Ephesians 5:18), we must first be emptied of ourselves. Jesus was clear on this: "If anyone would come after me, let him deny himself and take up his cross daily and follow me" (Luke 9:23). Then we can say with John the Baptist,

"[Jesus] must increase, but I must decrease" (John 3:30). And we will discover the truth of J. I. Packer's assertion: "You will never need more than he can supply."[3]

Yielding more of yourself to the Lord

The question is not the Spirit's ability but our availability. Oswald Chambers: "The true mark of the saint is that he can waive his own rights and obey the Lord Jesus." James Koester of the Society of Saint John the Evangelist notes: "It is when we live in union and communion with God that we can speak with the same authority as did Jesus. But knowing God, rather than knowing about God, is a dangerous thing. It requires us to be like Jesus. It requires us to empty ourselves and take on the form of a servant. It requires us to become obedient, even to the point of death. Only then can we say that we truly know God."[4] *Therefore, I urge you, brothers and sisters, in view of God's mercy, to offer your bodies as a living sacrifice, holy and pleasing to God—this is your true and proper worship. Do not conform to the pattern of this world, but be*

---

[3] Denison Forum, "William Barr's statement at Notre Dame: My perspective and God's call to courage" Oct. 15, 2019.

[4] Denison Forum, Oct. 15, 2019.

transformed by the renewing of your mind. Then you will be able to test and approve what God's will is—his good, pleasing and perfect will (Rom 12:1-2).

Abiding in Christ

You can achieve a lot on earth (in the realm of politics, science, music, art) even without Christ, and get the honor of men! A lot of preachers preach sermons without Christ! How do we know? Because they draw people unto themselves and not unto God. You can preach to get honor, to get admiration, and to get name or respect for yourself. Unfortunately, about 75% of Christians (in my guess) lack discernment to know the genuine men of God. They sit under a self-aggravating preacher and exclaim, 'waoo'! What a man of God!!! There will be surprises when Christ returns! (Matt 7:21-23). There are a lot of preachers on TV who perform magic and tricks to fool people—and on the last day, Christ will still say to them, 'away from me you workers of iniquities.'

Talking of something of eternal value, you cannot do anything except Christ enables you—You can do nothing of eternal value without the help of Christ (John 15:5). Whatever comes out of your self-confidence besides Christ will accompany nothing! The Apostle Paul said; "... *For it is we who are the circumcision, we who serve God by his Spirit, who boast in Christ Jesus, and who put no confidence in the flesh"* (Phil 3:3). After fifty years of bearing fruits, if a branch is cut off from the vine, it will bear zero fruit! In fact, it will dry off! This is why we need to be humble. Anything of eternal value that comes out from you comes out only by Christ pouring out His Spirit through you. People sometime pray when all other possibilities of solving the problem are gone. It is a wonderful thing to learn that we do not have to come to this desperate point before we rely on God! For instance, praying without ceasing means living a life of continuous dependence upon God! It is like a branch remaining attached to the tree all the time to bear fruit.

Abide in me and I abide in you—this is prayer without ceasing! This is a life of constant dependence on God inwardly even when we do not say it out with our mouths—Lord I know one thing that I cannot do anything without you that will last till eternity! Hence, humility is not to say, "I'm such a rotten sinner." Humility is to know and acknowledge that you can do nothing without Christ!" Jesus lived like this in all the days of his flesh on earth (John 5:19, 30). Jesus could do nothing without his Father! He came in the flesh and was 100% man when he was on earth! Hence, He depends totally on the Father! What about you? Power flow from Christ to us when we abide in him.

Seek no praise nor honor from men

Yet I do not receive testimony from man . . . (John 5:34). In life, people will definitely praise you if you perform well, but it becomes dangerous when you allow the praises of men to enter your head. Do not let the criticism from men hinder you from reaching your goal. Stop being moved by praise or criticism. If you listen too much to what people say about you, you will not hear what God is saying to you. Hence, the only reason why you are moved by the praise or criticism of men is simply because you are not dead to flesh yet. Have you ever seen a dead man responding to praises or criticism? No. Why? Because he is a dead man. Jesus said, "I do not receive honor from men" (John 5:41). It is the hypocrite that likes the praise of men more than the praise of God (John 5:43 paraphrase). In the same way, the apostles of old never sought men's praises. *"We were not looking for praise from people, not from you or anyone else"* (1 Thess 2:6). Beware of plastic praise of men!

Seek not the approval of men

In defense of his apostolic calling, the apostle remarked, "Am I now trying to win the approval of human beings, or of God? Or am I trying to please people? If I were still trying to please people, I would not be a servant of Christ" (Gal 1:10). The writer of Hebrews said, "There is no creature hidden from Him and everything is open and naked to Him with whom we have to do" (Hebrews 4:13). This is a lovely phrase; "Him with whom we have to do. According to Zac Poonen on this verse, it means that as believers (and regarding our spiritual journey), there is only one Person in the universe with whom we have to do, only One Person we are answerable to—God Himself. If you live your life recognizing this, you will become more and more godly. But if you are always thinking about the opinions that others have of you, you will become their slave throughout your life. If you want to be a servant of God, then recognize always that "it is only God with Whom you have to do." Ten thousand people calling you a godly person will not make you a godly person. In the same way, ten thousand people calling you an ungodly person will not make you ungodly. The Certificates from men are worthless. So, throw them all in the garbage bin—both good and bad opinions are equally fit for the garbage bin. Throw them there. If you do this, then, you will be freed to serve God.

Whatever you do, work at it with all your heart, as working for the Lord, not for human masters (Col 3:23; Eph 6:6). Christ once said to the Pharisees, "*You are the ones who justify yourselves in the eyes of others, but God knows your hearts. What people value highly is detestable in God's sight*" (Luke 16:15). On the contrary, we speak as those approved by God to be entrusted with the gospel. We are not trying to please people but God, who tests our hearts (1 Thess 2: 4).

Services in the church of God that are done to seek man's approval are clear expression of dead works. Deliver yourself from dead works as you render your duties to please Christ the Lord alone. The scriptures say, "how much more shall the blood of Christ, who through the eternal Spirit offered Himself without spot to God, cleanse your conscience from dead works to serve the living God? (Heb 9:14; cf 6:1).

Never seek to become men's pleaser in your life. I am sorry to say that Christendom has lost the understanding of what it means to be a servant of God. A true servant of God will not seek for any worldly honor nor the approval of men. Most Christian workers desire to sit on thrones and to get honor. Do not go that way; be a humble servant of God all your life. Be an ordinary brother or an ordinary sister, and even if you are rejected by the world and by the Babylonian Christendom as well, you will be accepted by the chief Shepherd—Jesus Christ our Lord and savior and he will fill you to an overflow with the Spirit.

Give thanks and praises to God continually

Have you noticed that the Lord's Prayer in Matt 6 begins with and ends with rendering praises and thanksgiving unto the Lord? Double check it again. A murmurer cannot enjoy the filling of God's presence. This is why the kingdom of God centers on righteousness, peace, and *joy in the Holy Spirit*. The Spirit of God does not dwell in the atmosphere of grumbling, murmuring, complaining and muddy look. The word of God says, delight yourself in the Lord, and he shall grant you the desire of your heart (Ps 37:4). If you want to build the atmosphere of heaven around you, develop an attitude of praises and thanksgiving in all situations (Ps 22: 3). There are no gloomy or sad angels in heaven—the hosts of heaven rejoice all the times. Remember to *"give thanks always for all things to God the Father in the name of our Lord Jesus Christ* (Eph 5:20). Similarly, 1 Thess 5: 18 says, *"give thanks in all circumstances; for this is God's will for you in Christ Jesus.*" The power of the Spirit of God flows freely where there is genuine praises going up to God. I remember several occasions that we (my wife and our prayer partners) have cast out demons without shouting but just praising God. Do not be anxious about anything, but in every situation, by prayer and petition, with thanksgiving, present your requests to God. When Jesus needed to feed thousands of people with few loaves of bread and two pieces of fish, he gave thanks and there was multiplication of the food. At the tomb of Lazarus, he gave thanks before commanding the spirit of death to lose its hold upon Lazarus (John 11: 41). Go and do likewise and you will experience the presence and power of God.

Always return Glory to God

No matter how God uses you, no matter how great the power of the Spirit that manifests through you, always remembers this; never share glory with God. He alone deserves all the glory and praises. I have seen the attitude of men that arrogate glory to themselves, and also see how they were cut short in their prime age in ministry and in life. I know a man of God sometime in the past that would always come in when songs of praises and worship were going on in the services. Whenever he and his wife stepped in to

242

enter (at the middle of the worship), the choristers and the congregation would stop the singing and start to eulogize him and his wife. Until the man of God and the first lady (his wife) would sit down majestically on their seats, then the singing continued. This is a dangerous path to tread. Be careful. Danger is looming when your followers can no longer reach God by themselves except through you. Danger is looming when you stand as intermediary between anyone and God. Do not take the role of Jesus the only mediator (1 Timothy 2:5). You are on a dangerous zone when your followers always quote your words than they quote the word of God—the Bible. It is becoming more dangerous for you when your followers can no longer live their lives or make decisions that have to do with their own lives, except they take permissions from you. When your followers fear and honor you the pastor more than they fear their parents or more than the reference they give to God, then, danger is looming. Be careful!

The same Holy Spirit who empowered Jesus during his earthly ministry (cf. Luke 4:14) and at his resurrection (1 Peter 3:18; Romans 8:11); empowered Peter's earthly ministry (Acts 2:4) and faithful death, he now dwells in us—we are his temple (1 Corinthians 3:16). He stands ready to use our spiritual giftings and manifest his spiritual fruit (Galatians 5:22–23) through us in our fallen culture to the glory of God the Father. It is time to become addicted seekers of God so as to launch ourselves into all that is available for us in this spiritual journey. *"He who has clean hands and a pure heart, who does not lift up his soul to an idol or swear deceitfully. He will receive blessing from the LORD and vindication from the God of his salvation.* **Such is the generation of those who seek Him, who seek Your face, O God of Jacob**" (Ps 24: 4-6). Again, a half-hearted seeker cannot experience all the fullness of God.

The spiritual dryness and drought continue to linger in our lives and our churches until we come under the outpouring of God's Spirit. The main reason why our churches are turning into deserts today is because; we have not been experiencing the rain of the Spirit of God presence and power. *"The palace and the city will be deserted, and busy towns will be empty. Wild donkeys will frolic and flocks will graze in the empty forts and watchtowers until at last the Spirit is poured out on us from heaven. Then the wilderness will become a fertile field, and the fertile field will yield bountiful crops. Justice will rule in the wilderness and righteousness in the fertile field"* (Isa 32: 14-16). On the day we begin to allow the flow of the power of the Holy Spirit of God in our congregations, the people shall be willing and serve God with gladness and joy (Ps 110: 3). The call still remains; *"If anyone thirsts, let him come to Me and drink. He who believes in Me, as the Scripture has said, out of his heart will flow rivers of living water"* (John 7: 37-38). Can you honestly say that the presence of the Spirit is flowing from you to the world around you like springs of living water? How thirsty are you for the power of the Holy Spirit? Without a daily intimacy of its adherents with the Holy Spirit, Christianity would be just another item on the list of the world's religious systems, consisting of mere traditions and rituals. The Christian life would be very boring and burdensome in the absence of a continuous encounter with the power of the Holy Spirit. The failure to receive the power of the Holy Spirit will not be a barrier to getting to heaven, but many of us may be amazed when we get to heaven and only to discover how much we ought to have done on earth for our Savior if we had yielded our lives to the power of His Spirit.

CPSIA information can be obtained
at www.ICGtesting.com
Printed in the USA
LVHW020303160721
692872LV00006B/109